IS BAD-FAITH
THE NEW WILFUL
BLINDNESS?

The Company Directors' Duty of Good Faith and Wilful
Blindness Doctrine Under Common Law USA (Delaware)
and UK (England): A Comparative Study

JO BAC

Author Photo by: Grant Triplow

Print information available on the last page.

ISBN: 978-1-4907-8437-3 (sc)
ISBN: 978-1-4907-8453-3 (e)

Trafford rev. 09/11/2017

Trafford PUBLISHING® www.trafford.com
North America & international
toll-free: 1 888 232 4444 (USA & Canada)
fax: 812 355 4082

TABLE OF CONTENTS

PART III – ENGLAND, UK

TABLE OF CASES

ABSTRACT

In the on-going financial and economic crisis in the United States of America (USA) and the United Kingdom (UK) this study poses a question as to whether company directors might have played a more active role in preventing the downfall. After corporate cataclysms such as WorldCom[1] and Enron[2], the questions of a uniform and unequivocal standard of directors' liability have become an urgent issue. The Enron and WorldCom scandals focused new attention on the misconduct of corporate officers. Chief Justice E. Norman Veasey warned in a speech that directors could have their behaviour 'treated as a breach of the

---

[1] WorldCom was the second biggest US long-distance phone company that filed for bankruptcy in 2002 after it revealed its executives inflated the company's assets by $11 billion. For more information, see D Thornburgh, 'A crisis in corporate governance? The Worldcom experience' (2006) <www.klgates.com/files/Publication/5ca1eda3-acd7-47e1-94316f0 511d1e7e4/Presentation/PublicationAttachment/ee2da30a-9843-4264 b182-f06d9d381051/Corp_Gov.pdf> accessed 17 August 2017.

[2] Enron was an American energy company based in Texas accompanied by massive fraud related to knowingly manipulating accounting rules. For more information, see The Economist, 'Enron. The Real Scandal. America's capital markets are not the paragons they were cracked up to be' (The Economist, 17 January 2002) <www.economist.com/node/940091> accessed 17 August 2017.

fiduciary duty of good faith.'[3] This study focus is on one particular corporate governance risk that arises from the similarities between traditional elements of a 'wilful blindness' cause of action, and those of company directors 'bad faith.'An essential aspect of any consideration of corporate governance is the role played by the directors of companies who might have been facilitating the wrongdoing, in part, by remaining 'wilfully blind' while falling foul of the 'good faith' obligation. This study investigates cross application of the doctrines of 'good faith' and 'wilful blindness' in Delaware, USA Company Law in comparison with England, UK Company Law with relation to company directors' conduct. Here is the argument that courts in both legal systems under a particular set of conditions and hearing cases of company directors falling foul of the 'good faith' obligation should consider whether the 'wilful blindness' doctrine sheds light on the interpretation of company directors' alleged misconduct. A positive consideration of this approach could expand the courts' horizons to include the most apparent individuals namely, the company directors to face liability concerns for corporate disasters.

---

[3] T Becker, 'Delaware Justice Warns of Board Liability for Executive Pay' (2003) A14 Wall Street Journal.

PART I

INTRODUCTION

CHAPTER 1

INTRODUCTION

'None of us knows what might happen even the next minute, yet still we go forward. Because we trust. Because we have Faith.'[4]

— Paulo Coelho, Brida

When a company violates the law, courts almost never find directors liable for breach of their fiduciary duties.[5] In the 2006 *Stone v. Ritter*[6] case the Delaware Supreme Court quoted Chancellor Allen's remark admitting that this type of claim against company directors is 'possibly the most difficult theory in corporation law upon which a plaintiff might hope to win a judgment.'[7] Correspondingly,

---

4   P Coelho, *Brida* (HarperCollins UK 2011).

5   See, for example, RT Miller, 'Wrongful Omissions by Corporate Directors: Stone v. Ritter and Adapting the Process Model of the Delaware Business Judgment Rule' (2008) 4 Journal of Business and Employment Law 951-954; BS Black, 'The Principal Fiduciary Duties of Boards of Directors' (2001) Presentation at Third Asian Roundtable on Corporate Governance Singapore, 4 April 2001.

6   *Stone v Ritter* 911 A2d 362 (Del 2006).

7   Ibid 371.

Linda Chatman Thomsen, the former Director of the Division of Enforcement, stated '[t]he commission rarely sues directors solely in their capacity as directors. In fact, in the last three years, during which we brought more than 1,800 enforcement actions involving more than 3,000 defendants and respondents, the commission has sued less than a dozen outside directors.'[8]

As a result, many contest that company directors should be personally liable for their mere omissions - not for considering an action and then deciding not to act, but 'for failing even to considering acting at all.'[9] They remind the business world, and especially its directors, that their appointments come with very real and important responsibilities and any breach of these responsibilities should act as grounds for the company directors' personal liability. Those remainders however, will not increase the number of directors sued for the breach of their duties as long as the courts struggle with the correct interpretation of company directors' conduct in relation to bad faith whether conscious, or wilfully blind.

A basic premise of this study is that the 'good faith' doctrine and the breach of the duty to act in 'good faith' should, to the extent possible, be analysed and defined by the courts, lawyers and scholars to resolve the uneasy situation involving cases of wrongful company directors' omissions. Focusing on the breach of the duty

---

[8] LC Thomsen, 'Speech by SEC Staff: Keeping up with the Smartest Guys in the Room: Raising the Bar for Corporate Boards' (*US Securities and Exchange Commission,* 12 May 2008) <www.sec.gov/news/speech/2008/spch051208lct.htm> accessed 17 August 2017.

[9] RT Miller, 'Wrongful Omissions by Corporate Directors: Stone v. Ritter and Adapting the Process Model of the Delaware Business Judgment Rule' (2008) 4 Journal of Business and Employment Law 952; Vince Cable, 'Transparency & Trust: Enhancing the transparency of UK company ownership and increasing trust in UK business' (*Gov.uk*, April 2014) <www.gov.uk/government/uploads/system/uploads/attachment_data/file/304297/bis-14-672-transparency-and-trust-consultation-response.pdf> accessed 17 August 2017.

of 'good faith' and mastering the process of its interpretation could achieve this aim. The author starts the process by turning to the etymology and substance of the 'good faith' doctrine and focuses on various courts and scholars' interpretations of this particular duty. This study during the process of its investigation finds existing links between the company directors' acts as falling foul of the duty to act in 'good faith', recklessness standards and the doctrine of 'wilful blindness' as promising grounds for further investigation.

This study contributes to the theory of company directors' duty to act in 'good faith' from the perspective of both corporate law jurisprudence in Delaware in the United States of America (USA) and England in the United Kingdom (UK).

Delaware has been chosen as a case study for this research, due to Black's argument that Delaware has become almost a 'brand name for "the business" of serving as the official home for corporations'.[10] This same supplying the business world with an adequate amount of statutory and case law is required in order to proceed with further investigation of this type of research. In addition, references to the federal law, which is applicable in Delaware, will be applied equally when necessary. English law has been chosen as a comparative case study for this research, due to Roberts' argument that London, with its latest UK Companies Act 2006[11] (the Act 2006), is a major European global business and financial centre.[12]

---

[10] LSB Black Jr, 'Why Corporation Choose Delaware (2007) Delaware Department of State' <http://corp.delaware.gov/pdfs/whycorporations_ english.pdf> accessed 17 August 2017. For more information, see MA Eisenberg, 'The Duty of Good Faith in Corporate Law' (2006) 31 Del J Corp L 1; AR Pinto and DM Branson, *Understanding Corporate Law* (LexisNexis 2013) 65.

[11] The Companies Act 2006 (c 46) <www.legislation.gov.uk/ukpga/2006/ 46/contents> accessed 17 August 2017.

[12] R Roberts, *The City: A Guide to London's Global Financial Centre* (John Wiley & Sons 2008). For more information, see Project Syndicate

1.1 Background to the Research and Findings – Delaware, USA

To begin with, this study's theory relies on the previous analysis of 'good faith' in Delaware articulated by Sale who puts forward the view that courts dealing with company directors who fail to act in 'good faith' ought to follow the lead of federal securities law, with a special focus on *scienter* under rule 10(b)-5 of the 1934 Securities Exchange Act. Professor Sale argues that '[u]nder such a standard, known or obvious infractions of corporate rules or governance standards, or failures to create such standards, would be actionable. Fiduciaries who fail to perform assigned tasks and to set up mechanisms to ensure that they are aware of such tasks would also be actionable. And, of course, 'good faith' reliance on the reports or information of others would still defeat such claims.'[13]

Scienter is a legal term that refers to the intent or knowledge of wrongdoing. This means that an offending party (e.g. a company director) has knowledge[14] of the 'wrongness' of an act or event prior to committing it.[15] Due to the federal courts' decisions, recklessness

---

economists, 'Will London survive as a financial centre after Brexit?' (*The Guardian*, 26 April 2017) <www.theguardian.com/business/2017/apr/26/london-financial-centre-brexit-eu-paris-frankfurt-uk> accessed 17 August 2017 where the authors argue that 'London will remain Europe's financial capital despite Brexit'.

[13] HA Sale, 'Delaware's Good Faith' (2004) 89 Cornell Law Review 456, 489-494.

[14] For the reasons of this study knowledge has been defined as not limited to positive knowledge, but includes the state of mind of one (e.g. company director) who does not possess positive knowledge only because he consciously avoided it. See, AH Loewy, *Criminal Law: Cases and Materials* (LexisNexis 2009).

[15] HH Pachecker, *Nafa's Blue Book: Legal Terminology, Commentaries, Tables and Useful Legal* (Publisher Xlibris Corporation 2010) 276; CTI Reviews, *The Legal and Regulatory Environment of Business: Business, Business law* (15th edn, CTI Reviews 2016).

has been chosen as an appropriate *scienter* requirement for federal securities fraud claims.[16] It is argued that Delaware courts have already employed standards from the federal securities law.[17] In the 1978 securities law case of *Roolf v Blyth, Eastman Dillon & Co., INC* the court held that '[it] is unquestionable that the common law has served as an interpretive source of securities law concepts'.[18]

Further analysis has led this study to the baseline concept of recklessness in common law and to the further examination of the relationship between recklessness understood as a *scienter* requirement in cases questioning company directors' conduct in relation to 'good faith'. In the 1964 federal securities law case of *United States v. Benjamin*[19] the court held that the defendant was reckless because he 'deliberately closed his eyes to facts [which] he had a duty to see'[20]. Subsequently, as argued by Edwards, this state of mind in deliberately closing one's eyes to events 'has generally been described as connivance or constructive knowledge, and approximates closely to the conception of recklessness'.[21]

---

[16] *Ottmann v Hanger Orthopedic Grp Inc* 353 F3d 338, 343 (4th Cir 2003) (citing various circuits' adoptions of recklessness as scienter for securities fraud) *Hudson v Phillips Petroleum Co (In re Phillips Petroleum Sec. Litig)* 881 F2d 1236, 1244 (3d Cir 1989); *Van Dyke v Coburn Enters* 873 F2d 1094, 1100 (8th Cir 1989); *McDonald v Alan Bush Brokerage Co* 863 F2d 809, 814 (11th Cir 1989); *Hackbart v Holmes* 675 F2d 1114, 1117-18 (10th Cir 1982); *Broad v Rockwell Int'l Corp* 642 F2d 929, 961-62 (5th Cir Apr 1981) (en banc); *Mansbach v Prescott, Ball Turben* 598 F2d 1017, 1023-25 (6th Cir 1979); *Sundstrand Corp v Sun Chem Corp* 553 F2d 1033, 1044-45 (7th Cir 1977); *Roolf v Blyth, Eastman Dillon & Co INC* 570 F2d 38, 45 (1978).

[17] *Rosenblatt v Getty Oil Co* 493 A2d 929 (1985).

[18] *Roolf v Blyth, Eastman Dillon & Co INC* 570 F2d 38, 45 (1978).

[19] *United States v Benjamin* 328 F2d 854, 861-63 (2d Cir 1964).

[20] Ibid 862.

[21] J Edwards, 'The Criminal Degrees of Knowledge' (1954) 17 Modern Law Review 294, 298. For more information, see J Herring, *Criminal Law: Text, Cases, and Materials* (Oxford University Press 2004) 170–172.

Many different terms denote the concept of deliberately 'closing one's eyes', including connivance, constructive knowledge or so-called 'wilful blindness' is a doctrine that originally has its roots in criminal law.[22] Heller and Dubber argue that 'wilful blindness' or so-called connivance is a form of subjective fault which has been interpreted as being the equivalent of knowledge.[23] Correspondingly, 'wilful blindness' arises when a person (e.g. company director) who has become aware of the need for some enquiry declines to make the enquiry because he/she does not want to take the responsibility for knowing the truth.[24] In line with the above, 'wilful blindness' is a theory of liability predicated on knowledge or rather a way of convicting those accused of offences (e.g. company directors) requiring a mens rea of knowledge.[25] As the author's further examination of this doctrine shows, 'wilful blindness' is not limited to criminal prosecutions. The analysis begins with an analogy from a recent civil enforcement case. As explained below, the court appeared to be increasingly aligning company directors' acts in civil proceedings with a doctrine of 'wilful blindness' originally having its roots in criminal law.[26] In February 2011 the US Securities

---

[22] See, for example, *Regina v Sleep* 169 Eng Rep 1296 (Cr Cas Res 1861); *Bosley v Davies* I QB 84 (1875); *Redgate v Haynes* I QB 89 (1876); *Spurr v United States* 174 US 728 (1899). For general information, see R Charlow, 'Wilful Ignorance and Criminal Culpability' (1992) 70 Tex L Rev 1351; RM Perkins, '"Knowledge" as a Mens Rea Requirement' (1978) 29 Hastings L 953, 956-57; IP Robbins, 'The Ostrich Instruction: Deliberate Ignorance as a Criminal Mens Rea' (1990) 813 Crim L & Criminology 191, 191.

[23] K Heller and M Dubber, *The Handbook of Comparative Criminal Law* (Stanford University Press 2010) 108.

[24] Ibid 108.

[25] SD Rodriguez, 'Caging Careless Birds: Examining Dangers Posed by the Willful Blindness Doctrine in the War on Terror' (2008) 30 U Pa J Int'l L 691, 714.

[26] As the discussion above attests.

and Exchange Commission[27] furthered this pattern by applying the 'wilful blindness' doctrine, borrowed from criminal law, to a recent civil enforcement case, when it sued three former directors of DHB Industries (DHB is a publicly-traded Delaware corporation), alleging that they 'were wilfully blind to numerous red flags[28] signalling accounting fraud, reporting violations and misappropriation at DHB. Instead, as the fraud swirled around them, they ignored the obvious and merely rubber-stamped the decisions of DHB's senior management while making substantial sums from sales of DHB's securities.'[29]

If courts truly intend to align 'bad faith' with other areas such as 'wilful blindness' in criminal law, as shown in the *SEC v Krantz* case,[30] this study considers that it would further have to extend that logic in deciding matters in related areas of the corporate. Indeed, during her investigation the author establishes that the acts of company directors in falling foul of the duty of 'good faith' in Delaware according to many scholars and courts have been closely related to the acts which involve recklessness or 'wilful blindness'.[31] Furthermore, some scholars, such as,

---

[27] The Securities and Exchange Commission oversees securities exchanges, securities brokers and dealers, investment advisors, and mutual funds in an effort to promote fair dealing, the disclosure of important market information, and to prevent fraud. <www.sec.gov> accessed 17 August 2017.

[28] The Red Flags Rule (RFR) is a set of United States federal regulations that require certain businesses and organisations to develop and implement documented plans to protect consumers from identity theft. Red Flag Program Clarification Act of 2010 (S.3987) <www.gpo.gov/fdsys/browse/collection.action?collectionCode=BILLS> accessed 17 August 2017.

[29] *SEC v Krantz* et al case 0:11-cv-60432 [SD Fla].

[30] Ibid.

[31] *David B Shaev Profit Sharing Account v Armstrong CA* No 1449-N 2006 WL 391931 at 1* (Del Ch Feb 13 2006); EN Veasey, 'State-Federal Tension in Corporate Governance and the Professional Responsibilities

for example, Edwards, have been deliberately cross - applying recklessness with 'wilful blindness'.[32] Which is in line with the reasoning of the US Court of Appeals for the Third Circuit (in case citations, 3d Cir.) which is a federal court with appellate jurisdiction over the district courts for the district of Delaware.[33] When looking to different areas of Delaware law, it became apparent that 'knowledge' may be interpreted to mean (1) actual knowledge; (2) recklessness or reckless disregard; or (3) 'wilful blindness'.

Accordingly, this study considers the meaning and viability of 'wilful blindness' for claims of falling foul of the duty of 'good faith', while also considering 'wilful blindness' and higher levels of knowledge as possible standards for *scienter*. This is to argue further that the interpretation of the acts of company directors in falling foul of the duty of 'good faith' in Delaware under a particular set of circumstances should follow the direction of a theory of 'wilful blindness' standard that might be found in case law and the Model Penal Code.[34]

The next part considers the background to the research of the company directors' duty to act in 'good faith' in the best interest of the company in England, UK.

---

of Advisors' (2003) 28 J Corp L 441, 447; HA Sale, 'Delaware's Good Faith' (2004) 89 Cornell Law Review 456 and J Edwards, 'The Criminal Degrees of Knowledge' (1954) 17 Modern Law Review 294, 298.

[32] Ibid (n 18) 98.

[33] *United States v Stadtmauer* 620 F 3d 238, 253 (3rd Cir 2010).

[34] Model Penal Code: A proposed criminal code drafted by the American Law Institute that states may choose to adopt as their criminal law. Some states have adopted the Model Penal Code in its entirety as their criminal law others have adopted parts of the Model Penal Code (e.g. Delaware); while some states have completely ignored it. For more information see: MD Dubber, *Criminal Law: Model Penal Code* (Foundation Press 2002).

1.2 Background to the Research and Findings – England, UK

Keay points out that an essential aspect of any consideration of corporate governance is the role played by the directors of companies.[35] Directors are made accountable for how they have conducted the affairs of their company. Hence, similarly as with regard to the Delaware jurisprudence certain duties are imposed in England on how directors act in the management of their companies' affairs. If the company directors fail to fulfil their duties, they may be subject to legal proceedings and held liable by the courts.[36] After many years when directors' duties in England were provided for by common law rules and equitable principles, England has followed other common law jurisdictions and has codified the duties in the Act 2006, principally Chapter 2 of Part 10 of that statute.[37] The duty upon which the study focuses is that contained in section 172 (1) of the Act 2006. It provides that:

> 'A director of a company must act in a way that he considers, in 'good faith', would be most likely to promote the success of the company for the benefit of its members as a whole (...)'[38]

This section has been in force for almost few years but there is little or no relevant case law to ascertain how section 172(1) might

---

[35] A Keay, 'The Duty to Promote the Success of the Company: Is It for Purpose?' (2010) University of Leeds School of Law, Centre for Business Law and Practice Working Paper <http://ssrn.com/abstract=1662411> accessed on 17 August 2017.

[36] See, for example, J Loughrey (ed), *Directors' Duties and Shareholder Litigation in the Wake of the Financial Crisis* (Edward Elgar Publishing 2013) 53.

[37] Ibid (n 8) Chapter 2 Part 10.

[38] Ibid (n 8) section 172 (1).

be interpreted and viewed by courts. The concept of 'good faith' remains 'either novel or elusive.' [39] As established by this research, both case law and statutory law indicate that, for most of the time, the courts would conclude that company directors are acting in 'good faith', unless the plaintiff can show evidence to show that they are not, or unless the company directors' actions were so unreasonable that no reasonable person would have done the same thing in that situation.[40] Arguably, and corresponding to the case of the Delaware case scenario, reasonableness or the reasonable person could potentially define the act of 'good faith' in English company law. This suggestion has been followed by this study with a brief look at reasonableness from the common law perspective.

A reasonable person has been defined as motivated by a wish for a social world in which they are free and equal, and which is able to act together with others on terms which all can accept, so that each benefits along with the others.[41] The author differentiates the rational company director, who acts in a way that is the best for his/her personal situation, from the reasonable company director, who takes a proper interest in company affairs and acts in the best interests of the company.

Following Luntz, Hambly and Hayes this study recognizes that the standard of the reasonable person most of the time is an idealised and ethical one, rather than the conduct of the actual 'man in the street'.[42] As pointed out by Wierzbicka, any court's knowledge which is based on the hypothetical judgment of a

---

[39] TL Anderson and R Sousa, *Reacting to the Spending Spree: Policy Changes We Can Afford* (Hoover Press 2013) 93. Also, see R Brownsword, *Good Faith in Contract: Concept and Context* (Ashgate Publishing Group 1999) where the author argues: '[g]ood faith is an elusive idea, taking on different meanings from one context to another'.

[40] See, for example, *Charterbridge Corp Ltd v Lloyds Bank Ltd* [1970] Ch 62.

[41] J Rawls, *Political Liberalism* (Columbia University Press 1993) 50.

[42] H Luntz and D Hambly and R Hayes, *Torts: Cases and Commentary* (Butterworths 1985).

reasonable person can be analysed or interpreted as 'probabilistic, limited, and fallible'.[43] Interestingly for this study, however, in the 1970 company law case of *Charterbridge Corp Ltd v Lloyds Bank Ltd*[44] his Lordship Pennycuick J stated that the proper test while questioning the company director's acts of 'good faith' is when an intelligent and honest man in the position of a director of the company concerned, could in the existing circumstances, have reasonably believed that the transaction was in the best interests of the company.[45] As a consequence the author argues that a person who acts against the duty of 'good faith' could be described as an unreasonable and 'dishonest man'.

As stated in the introductory section to the Delaware law, while emphasising USA company directors' duty to act in 'good faith', it has even included recklessness.[46] 'There is nothing to suggest, however, that the [English] UK jurisprudence has gone that far'[47]. This study acquiesces with this view though with the addendum that 'good faith' or rather falling foul of the obligation of 'good faith' from the perspective of the company directors' conduct in English jurisprudence may go as far as acts of dishonesty of the party in question. This in turn might provide a direct connection with the 'wilful blindness' doctrine. The present author recognizes and maintains that this might be the case only under a particular set of circumstances. As found by this study the specific circumstances in which the company directors' duty of 'good faith' or, rather, falling foul of the duty to act in 'good faith' may be cross applied with the 'wilful blindness' doctrine

---

[43] A Wierzbicka, *English: Meaning and Culture* (Oxford University Press 2006) 108.

[44] *Charterbridge Corpn Ltd v Lloyds Bank Ltd* [1970] Ch 62.

[45] Ibid 74.

[46] As the discussion above attests.

[47] A Keay, *The Enlightened Shareholder Value Principle and Corporate Governance* (Routledge 2012) 95.

in English jurisprudence have been embedded in dishonest assistance[48] case law.

With regard to the dishonest assistance case law there are two requirements for the defendant's (e.g. company director's) liability. The first one is that the defendant must have assisted in the breach of trust and that the breach of trust shall stand for a breach of any fiduciary duty.[49] The second condition is that the defendant's assistance must have been dishonest.[50] The author finds that in a dishonest assistance law case in 1995 cited as *Royal Brunei Airlines Sdn Bhd v Tan*[51] Lord Nicholls stated that an honest person does not 'deliberately close his eyes and ears, or deliberately not ask questions, lest he learn something he would rather not know, and then proceed regardless'[52]. Likewise, in the 2002 trust law case of *Twinsectra Ltd v Yardley*[53], Lord Slynn held that 'prima facie, shutting one's eyes to problems or implications and not following them up may well indicate dishonesty.[54] This study argues that the same conditions of the 'dishonest' test are required when questioning whether company directors' acts of

---

[48] Company directors owe duties to their company including fiduciary duties based on their office as director. The general rule is that company directors owe no fiduciary duty to a beneficiary of a trust which owns the share in the company. However one of the exceptions to that rule is that the remedy of dishonest assistance is available to beneficiaries against directors who act dishonestly in causing the company to commit, or otherwise assist the company to commit, a breach of trust. For more see: A Halpin, *Definition in the Criminal Law* (Hart Publishing 2004) 158.

[49] For ease of reference the term 'breach of trust' shall stand for 'breach of any fiduciary duty', and the term 'beneficiary' shall stand for 'any purposes who takes a benefit from any fiduciary duty'; See: *Dubai Aluminium v Salaam* [2002] 3 WLR 1913; [2003] 1 All ER 97 para 9.

[50] Ibid (n 37).

[51] *Royal Brunei Airlines Sdn Bhd v Tan* [1995]2 AC 378.

[52] Ibid.

[53] *Twinsectra Ltd v Yardley* [2002] UKHL 12.

[54] Ibid 4.

'good faith' are in the best interest of the company and while testing defendants in dishonest assistance cases. This study argues further that the grounds or the foundations which the 'dishonest' test have been based upon constitute the 'wilful blindness' doctrine. Consequently, this study concludes, that the English company directors' dishonest breach of the duty to act in 'good faith' in the best interest of the company in question can be cross-applied to acts of 'wilful blindness' under English jurisprudence.

1.3 Research Design

The research design used in this project is a quantitative descriptive design because it discusses and analyses data relating to company directors' duty to act in 'good faith' and in the best interests of the company as well as the 'wilful blindness' doctrine in terms of journals, books, legal cases and acts in Delaware, USA and England, UK. This research methodology required the author to gather relevant data from the specified acts, case law, books, journal articles and on-line sources and analyse the material in order to arrive at a more complete understanding of company directors' duty to act in 'good faith' and the possibility of its cross application with the doctrine of 'wilful blindness' in Delaware, USA and England, UK.

1.4 Research Questions

The author sheds light on the following questions throughout the research:

1) How did company directors' duty of 'good faith' historically manifest itself in Delaware, USA and in England, UK and how does it manifest itself currently?

2) What are the different ways to interpret falling foul of the duty to act in 'good faith' in respect of the company directors' conduct in Delaware, USA and England, UK?

3) Can the doctrine of 'wilful blindness' which originates in criminal law be applied to civil (non-criminal) proceedings? If the answer is "yes", what are the civil proceedings to which the doctrine of 'wilful blindness' can be applied?

4) To what extent can the doctrine of 'good faith' in relation to company directors' conduct be cross applied with the doctrine of 'wilful blindness' in Delaware, USA and in England, UK?

5) What are the particular circumstances which are required to enable the cross-application between the doctrines of 'good faith' and 'wilful blindness' in relation to the company directors' conduct in both Delaware, USA and in England, UK?

Contributions of the study

This study adds value to the field of corporate governance in both Delaware, USA and England, UK and related areas of study, like corporate directors' duty of acting in 'good faith', the relation between 'good faith' and 'wilful blindness' doctrines at a theoretical as well as a methodological level. Firstly, insight into the world of directors' duty of 'good faith' will contribute to our knowledge of this phenomenon. In particular, it will illuminate the similarities between breaching the duty of 'good faith' and actions of 'wilful blindness'. This is turn is designed to provide answer to whether the similarities between them may lead judicial decisions to suggest that 'wilful blindness' can be applied in limited ways — to situations involving something similar to actual knowledge of the relevant facts, and deliberate action to avoid confirming a high likelihood of wrongdoing. Secondly, applying qualitative methods will introduce qualitative methodology to the study of corporate directors duty of 'good faith', actions of bad faith and 'wilful blindness' in the general field of corporate governance. Thirdly, this correlative constitution of a field of knowledge between 'bad faith' in directors' conduct and 'wilful blindness' may create a framework to facilitate the improvement of corporate governance.

1.5 Book Outline

To assist the reader in further exploration of this topic Part II and its Chapter 2 focuses on the grounding principles of Delaware law. Chapter 3 elaborates on development of the company directors' duty to act in 'good faith' under Delaware statute and case law. Chapter 4 comments on the subject of the recklessness standard under common law and discusses the case for aligning the company directors breaching the duty of 'good faith' with recklessness. Chapter 5 provides the reader with discussion on the 'wilful blindness' doctrine under Delaware law and discusses the case for aligning the company directors breaching the duty of 'good faith' with 'wilful blindness'. Part III takes the perspective of English jurisprudence. Chapter 6 focuses on the grounding principles of English law with relation to the 'good faith' doctrine and elaborates on development of the company directors' duty to act in 'good faith'. Chapter 7 provides the reader with discussion on the reasonableness and honesty man under English Law and discusses the case for aligning the company directors' duty of 'good faith' with acts of reasonableness and honesty. Chapter 8 comments on the subject of the 'wilful blindness' where he author argues that Under English jurisprudence the doctrines' cross-application is possible in the company directors' dishonest assistance cases.

Part IV concludes the findings.

PART II

DELAWARE, USA

CHAPTER 2

DELAWARE LAW

2.1 Guiding Principles of Delaware Law

Delaware continues to be the favoured state of incorporation for USA businesses and through its developed legal system and laws protecting shareholders' and board of directors' rights having a reputation as being a haven for corporations.[55] The Delaware Court of Chancery [56], together with the State Supreme Court[57],

---

[55] See, for example, TL Hazen and JW Markham, *Corporations and Other Business Enterprises* (West 2003) 165; L Wayne, 'How Delaware Thrives as a Corporate Tax Haven' (*The NY Times*, 30 June 2012) <www.nytimes.com/2012/07/01/business/how-delaware-thrives-as-a-corporate-tax-haven.html> accessed 17 August 2017; Usa Ibp Usa (ed), *Us Company Laws and Regulations Handbook Volume 2 Delaware - Corporate Laws and Regulation in the Selected States of the Us Delaware* (Int'l Business Publications 2009) 48.

[56] Delaware Court of Chancery is a court of equity in the American state of Delaware. It is one of Delaware's three constitutional courts, along with the Supreme Court and Superior Court. <http://courts.delaware.gov/chancery/> accessed 17 August 2017.

[57] Supreme Court of Delaware is the sole appellate court in the United States' state of Delaware <http://courts.delaware.gov/supreme/index.stm> accessed 17 August 2017.

has developed a worldwide reputation as a respected source of legal decisions[58] and this state's General Corporation Law (hereafter referred to as 'DGCL')[59] is said to have the most advanced and flexible corporation statutes in the USA nation.[60] Arguably, Delaware has a better-developed body of statutory and case law than any other state hence might serve to give this research greater guidance on matters relevant to any company directors' duty including the duty to act in 'good faith.'

2.2 Delaware General Corporation Law

DGCL is the statute governing corporate law in the USA state of Delaware which permits corporations and their shareholders the maximum flexibility when ordering their affairs. It does not appear to be a code of conduct. Instead, it is written with a bias against regulation.[61] This is exactly the statute that uses the term 'good faith' in several instances and approximately 17 times to describe the state of mind required of a company director, aiming to use powers that have been granted by this statute.[62] The business of a Delaware corporation is managed by the leadership of its board of directors which has the powers of delegation.[63] In the 1985 corporate law case of *Rosenblatt v. Getty Oil Co.,* the court held that an informed decision to delegate a piece of business is as much an

---

[58] LSB Black Jr (n 10).

[59] Delaware General Corporation Law (Title 8, Chapter 1 of the Delaware Code) <http://delcode.delaware.gov/title8/c001/index.shtml> accessed 17 August 2017.

[60] LSB Black Jr, 'Why Corporation Choose Delaware' (*Delaware Department of State* 2007) <http://corp.delaware.gov/pdfs/whycorporations_english. pdf> accessed 17 August 2017; RA Mann and BS Roberts, *Essentials of Business Law and the Legal Environment* (Cengage Learning 2012) 619.

[61] LSB Black Jr (n 10) 3.

[62] Ibid.

[63] Ibid (n 59) § 141(a).

activity of business judgment as any other.[64] In the corporate law case of *Aronson v. Lewis* in 1984 the court held that the business judgment rule (hereafter referred to as 'BJR') allows courts to presume that, in making business decisions, company directors act in having or showing knowledge of a subject or situation basis while acting in 'good faith' and in the honest belief that the action taken was in the company's best interest.[65]

For the BJR to apply, however, three pre-conditions must be met: care, loyalty and independence. If these elements are found, the substantive decision, whether good or bad with the benefit of hindsight, will be sustained if it can be attributed to a rational business purpose.[66] BJR empowers company directors who are not influenced by considerations of personal advantage and who are free from outside control with an important state of physical ease and freedom from being held liable to stockholders as a result of their business decisions.

In the 1985 corporate law case of *Smith v. Van Gorkom* that will be analysed further, the Delaware Supreme Court found a board of directors personally liable for their breach of the duty of care in deciding to sell the company to a third party without exploring available alternatives or a factual framework.[67] The *Van Gorkom* created distress among company directors followed by the Delaware General Assembly[68] enacting Section 102(b)(7) of the DGCL. This was of a great relevance to the statutory basis of 'good faith'. Section 102(b)(7) was the legislature's affirmation of the

---

[64]   *Rosenblatt v Getty Oil Co* 493 A2d 929, 943 (Del 1985).

[65]   *Aronson v Lewis* 473 A2d 805, 812 (Del 1984).

[66]   S Judge, *Q & A Revision Guide: Company Law 2012 and 2013* (Oxford University Press 2012) 142.

[67]   *Smith v Van Gorkom* 488 A2d 585, 868-69 (Del 1985).

[68]   The Delaware General Assembly is the legislature of the US state of Delaware. It is a bicameral legislature: the Delaware Senate with 21 Senators and the Delaware House of Representatives with 41 Representatives <http://openstates.org/de/> accessed on 17 August 2017.

principle that the judiciary would stay out of company directors' conduct, provided that the board did not behave disloyally or, as the statute added, in bad-faith.

The courts' opinions each provide the same two non-exclusive examples of what would be lack of good faith: (a) where the company director acts with the intention to violate applicable positive law and/or (b) where the company director intentionally fails to act in the face of a known duty to act, indicating a conscious disregard for his/her duties. [69] In addition, section 8.30 of the Model Business Corporation Act, and which has been adopted in Delaware, provides that '[e]ach member of the board of directors, when discharging the duties of a director, shall act (...) in "good faith".'[70] Still, the exact meaning behind the doctrine of 'good faith' was left undefined.

---

[69]   *Stone v Ritter* 911 A2d 362 (Del 2006); *In re Walt Disney Co Derivative Litigation* 906 A 2d 27 (Del 2006); *In re Walt Disney Derivative Litigation* 907 A 2d 693 (2005).

[70]   Section 8.30 of the Model Business Corporation Act.

CHAPTER 3

————•❰❰❰❱❱❱•————

GOOD FAITH IN DELAWARE

3.1 Overview of Company Directors' Duty of Good Faith

Some scholars and courts argue that the duty of 'good faith' in relation to company directors' conduct constitutes a specific set of obligations which consist of company directors' honesty, or sincerity; non-contravention of decency applicable to the conduct of business; non-contravention of commonly accepted basic company norms and loyalty to the office.[71] In summary, 'good faith is used as a loose rhetorical device that courts can wield to find liability to enjoin actions that do not quite fit within established doctrinal categories'[72] and no one is able to provide a concise definition of this term.[73] Nowicki indicates even that 'judicial attempts to enforce a director's obligation to act in 'good

---

[71] MA Eisenberg, The Duty of Good Faith in Corporate Law (2006) 31 Delaware Journal of Law 5.

[72] SJ Griffith, 'Good Faith Business Judgment: A Theory of Rhetoric in Corporate Law Jurisprudence' (2005) 55 Duke L J 1, 34.

[73] See, for example, HN Butler and LE Ribstein, 'Opting Out of Fiduciary Duties: A Response to the Anti- Contractarians' (1990) 65 WASH L

faith' - what [she] refers to as the "bastardization of the phrase, 'not in "good faith"'-fall away as merely restrictions on directors acting affirmatively in bad faith.'[74] She continues 'the attempts of other scholars to propound on "good faith" seem to only be focused on understanding what the courts are doing, as opposed to guiding what the judiciary should be doing.'[75] In the 1999-company case law *Jackson Nat'l Life Ins. Co. v. Kennedy*, Vice Chancellor Steele left 'it to the [Delaware] Supreme Court and to the academic community to distinguish the fiduciary duties of loyalty and "good faith".'[76] Delaware courts frequently refer to a company director's duty of 'good faith'[77] and find it equally challenging to state the exact nature of this particular duty.[78] For example, in 2005, in the corporate law case of *Walt Disney Co. Derivative Litig (Disney IV)*, the judge even defined his struggle as a 'fog of hazy jurisprudence'[79]. Not discouraged by this challenge the next section of this study sheds some light on the legal status, the etymology, historical development, and case law justifications of and meanings behind this duty.

REV 1; FH Easterbrook and DR Fischel, Contract and Fiduciary Duty (1993) 36 J L & ECON 425.

[74] EA Nowicki, 'A Director's Good Faith' (2007) 55 Buff L Rev 457, 457.

[75] Ibid.

[76] *Jackson Nat'l Life Ins Co v Kennedy* 741 A 2d 377, 389 n 18 (Del Ch 1999).

[77] See, for example, *Aronson v Lewis* 473 A2d 805, 812 (Del 1984); *Brehm v Eisner* 746 A2d 244 (Del 2000); *Cede & Co v Technicolor, Inc* (Cede II) 634 A2d 345, 361 (Del 1993).

[78] Cede II, 634 A2d at 361–66 (presenting sections on the duty of loyalty and the duty of care, but not containing definition on good faith).

[79] *Walt Disney Co Derivative Litig* (Disney IV) 907 A2d 693, 754 (Del Ch 2005).

3.2 Good Faith - Company Statutes, Fiduciary Duties & Etymology

First, the duty of 'good faith' has achieved permanent recognition in company statutes.[80] Many company statutes express the obligation of company directors to act in 'good faith'. For example, NY Business Corporation Law L § 717 (2014) 717 states: '(a) A director shall perform his duties as a director, including his duties as a member of any committee of the board upon which he may serve, in 'good faith' and with that degree of care which an ordinarily prudent person in a like position would use under similar circumstances.[81] Model Business Corporation Act Subchapter C. Standards of Conduct §8.30 General Standards for Directors (a) A director shall discharge his duties as a director, including his duties as a member of a committee: (1) in 'good faith'.[82] The Delaware General Corporation Law (the "DGCL") Section 102(b)(7) expressly provides that directors cannot be protected from liability '(ii) for acts or omissions not in 'good faith' or which involve intentional misconduct or a knowing violation of law'.[83]

Second, the duty of 'good faith' has a long history in company directors' fiduciary obligations, which means that company directors have the duty to act with loyalty and care.[84] In 1993 the corporate law case of *Rales v. Blasband* proclaimed that the duty to act with loyalty refers to company directors being involved in transactions with the company and receiving a personal financial benefit from a transaction that is not equally

---

[80] CW Furlow, 'Good Faith, Fiduciary Duties and the Business Judgment Rule in Delaware' (2009) Utah Law Review 1061.

[81] NY Bus Corp L § 717 (2014) 717 (a) Duty of directors.

[82] MBCA § 8.30.

[83] The Delaware General Corporation Law Section 102(b)(7).

[84] *Walt Disney Co Derivative Litig* 825 A2d 275, 286 (2003).

shared by the stockholders.[85] Some scholars suggest that the duty of loyalty has played an important defining role in relation to the duty of 'good faith'. Here, the author turns to the third premise on how to define the duty of 'good faith' – etymology. After all loyalty[86], fidelity[87] and faithful[88] are all synonyms. Strine sees that a common way to describe a disloyal company director is as a 'faithless fiduciary'.[89] To be 'faithless' means to be 'disloyal'[90] and it would be very difficult to disconnect those themes. Furthermore, 'faith' has its roots in the Latin word 'fides' which means a person 'that stands in a special relation of trust, confidence, or responsibility in certain obligations to others'.[91] 'Faith' together with 'good' carries an unbreakable relationship between the concepts of 'fidelity' and 'loyalty'. Therefore, in a company context, an action undertaken in 'good faith' by the company directors means an action undertaken which is consistent with their duty, for a faithful and loyal purpose.

---

85 *Rales v Blasband* 634 A2d 927, 936 (Del 1993).

86 'The etymological origins of loyal and loyalty can be traced to the Old French leial, which originally was from the Latin legalis, or legal, and lex, or law, and then became loyal'; *American Heritage Dictionary of the English Language* (4th edn, Houghton Mifflin Harcourt 2000) 1038.

87 'It traces the origin of the word to the Latin, fidelis, or faithful, which came from the Latin fides, or faith'; *American Heritage Dictionary of the English Language* (4th edn, Houghton Mifflin Harcourt 2000) 655.

88 '[f]aithful and loyal both suggest undeviating attachment'; *American Heritage Dictionary of the English Language* (4th edn, Houghton Mifflin Harcourt 2000) 636.

89 LE Strine Jr, 'Can We Do Better by Ordinary Investors? A Pragmatic Reaction to the Dueling Ideological Mythologists of Corporate Law' (2014) 2(114) Columbia Law Review 449.

90 RL Cherry, *Title English Words: From Latin and Greek Elements* (University of Arizona Press 1986) 84.

91 *American Heritage Dictionary of the English Language* (Houghton Mifflin Harcourt 2000).

3.3 Historical Development of the Company Directors' Duty of Good Faith under Case Law

In the 1985 corporate law case of *Smith v. Van Gorko,* the Delaware Supreme Court found a board of directors personally liable for approving a merger agreement without substantial inquiry or any expert advice.[92] In the Court's opinion, this reckless behaviour amounted to gross negligence[93] and breach of a duty of care.[94] The agreement proved to produce a great deal of profit for the shareholders; therefore, as argued by Bergman and Cox, many business leaders described the Court's decision as injudicious.[95] As a consequence of the judgment in *Smith v. Van Gorkom* case, the Delaware legislature added section 102(b)(7) to the DGCL, which states '[a] provision eliminating or limiting the personal liability of a director to the corporation or its stockholders for monetary damages for breach of fiduciary duty as a director, provided that such provision shall not eliminate or limit the liability of a director: (ii) for acts or omissions not in 'good faith' or which involve intentional misconduct or a knowing violation of law.' [96] The duty of 'good faith' has become increasingly important because the liability of company directors for violation of the duty of 'good faith' could not be waived.[97]

---

[92]   *Smith v Van Gorkom* 488 A2d 858, 863 (Del 1985).

[93]   Gross negligence is legal concept which means serious carelessness. For more information, see WP Keeton, *Prosser and Keeton on the Law of Torts* (5th edn, West Group 1984) 34.

[94]   Ibid (n 36).

[95]   DA Burgman and PN Cox, DA and Cox, PN, 'Corporate Directors, Corporate Realities and Deliberative Process: An analisis of the Trans Union Case' (1986) 11 Journal of Corporation Law 311, 333.

[96]   Delaware General Corporation Law section 102(b)(7) <http://delcode. delaware.gov/title8/c001/> accessed 17 August 2017.

[97]   Ibid.

Over the next few years, Delaware jurisprudence has been indistinct on the issue of 'good faith'. In the 1993, corporate law case of *Cede & Co. v. Technicolor, Inc.* *('Technicolor')*, the Delaware Supreme Court denoted for the first time in the history that company directors owe a 'triad' of fiduciary duties.[98] Apart from the duty of loyalty and the duty of care, the duty of 'good faith' has been imposed on company directors. The duty of 'good faith' requires that directors act honestly, in the best interest of the corporation, and in a manner that is not knowingly unlawful or contrary to public policy.[99] Still, this case just referred to 'good faith' without providing any guidance as to what the duty might necessitate.

3.3.1 *In re the Walt Disney Co Derivative Litigation,* 825 A 2d 275 (Del Ch 2003)

The *Disney* cases[100] confirm the intermediate standard between loyalty and care which is the duty of 'good faith'. One of the most significant court decisions with regard to the company directors' duty to act in 'good faith' can be found in the 2003 corporate law case *In re Walt Disney Co. Derivative Litigation* case *('Disney III')*[101]. This is actually the first case that required the Delaware

---

[98] *Cede & Co v Technicolor Inc* 634 A2d 345, 361 (Del 1993).

[99] Ibid.

[100] When this study turns to the Disney case it recognizes it as a collective reference to all the opinions both in the Supreme Court of Delaware and in the Chancery Court. The first opinion was *In re the Walt Disney Co Derivative Litigation* 731 A 2d 342 (Del Ch 1998) ('In re Disney Derivative Litigation'). The appeal was *Brehm v Eisner* 746 A 2d 244 (Del 2000) ('Disney II'), granting plaintiffs leave to replead in part. Following the appeal, *In re the Walt Disney Co Derivative Litigation*, 825 A 2d 275 (Del Ch 2003) ('In re Disney Litigation' or 'Disney III'), dealt with the motion to dismiss the amended complaint, which was denied.

[101] *In re The Walt Disney Co Deriv Litig*, 825 A2d 275 (Del Ch 2003) ('Disney III').

court to give their proper attention to this duty and recognize it as self-sufficient for launching proceedings in a civil action. The background of this procedure is described in detail here.

Sparks, Hurd and Hirzel are of the view that Michael Ovits became one of the most important people in Hollywood when Disney's Michael Eisner, had offered him the position as the company's president after the sad death of Frank Wells, the company's former president.[102] Eisner and the chairman of Disney's compensation committee, Irwin Russell, on behalf of the company reached an agreement with Ovitz under which Ovitz was supposed to gain a five-year contract. Not long thereafter, Ovitz was presented with a severance agreement. Griffith has argued that the main error in the negotiation of this employment agreement was in initiating Ovitz to expect a no-fault termination instead of looking for a long-term relationship with the company.[103] Ovitz left the company after fifteen months with approximately 140 million American dollars in stock and cash.[104] Unhappy shareholders sued the directors and officers alleging that they had breached their fiduciary duties with respect to the hiring and dismissing of Ovitz.

In 1998, the Court of Chancery initially dismissed the case (*In re Walt Disney Co Derivative Litig*, 731 A2d 342, 380 (Del Ch 1998)).[105] However, in 2000, the case reached the Delaware Supreme Court as an appeal in *Brehm v. Eisner ('Disney II')*[106]. On

---

[102] AG Sparks and SM Hurd and ST Hirzel, 'Good Faith and the Walt Disney Company Derivative Litigation - Guidance for Directors of Delaware Corporations' <www.nacdfl.org/Portals/0/Outline%20%20 Good%20Faith%20and%20The%20Walt%20Disney%20Co.pdf> accessed 17 August 2017.

[103] SJ Griffith, 'Good Faith Business Judgment: A Theory of Rhetoric in Corporate Law Jurisprudence' (2005) 55(1) Duke Law Journal 1–69.

[104] *Unsecured Creditors of Integrated Health Services, Inc v Elkins* CA No 20228-NC, 2004 Del Ch LEXIS 122 (Del Ch August 24, 2004).

[105] *In re Walt Disney Co Derivative Litig*, 731 A2d 342, 380 (Del Ch 1998).

[106] *Brehm v Eisner* 746 A2d 244 (Del 2000) ('Disney II').

appeal, the Delaware Supreme Court upheld the dismissal of the original complaint for a failure to make demand to the board. The Delaware Supreme Court argued that the complaint did not raise a reasonable doubt about whether the directors were neutral or uncommitted or should not be protected by the business judgment rule.[107] Nonetheless, the Supreme Court afforded the plaintiffs with an opportunity to plead their demand again and bring the case to the Court of Chancery.

The plaintiffs did so in 2003 in the so-called *Disney III* case.[108] At this point, however, the complaint was amended by stripping it from the duty of loyalty claim. Without having an argument under the duty of loyalty, the plaintiffs were left with only a duty of care claim which left the Disney company with the DGCL 102(b)(7) provision. This provision was empowering the board of directors to exempt claims rising solely under the duty of care.[109] Unfortunately, without the loyalty component, the claim faced the prospect of another dismissal. Fortunately for the plaintiffs, Chancellor Chandler referred to the duty of 'good faith' in order to save their case and argued that the plaintiffs had advocated 'particularized facts sufficient to raise (...) a reason to doubt that the action was taken honestly and in "good faith"'.[110]

It was for the second time[111] in the history of the Delaware Courts that the duty of 'good faith' had been given an independent doctrinal effect, being separate and unconnected from both duty of loyalty and duty of care. This was simply because the plaintiffs' claim would be invalid under any of the traditional fiduciary duties. There was no basis under the duty of loyalty because it had not been raised on appeal and no basis under the duty of care

---

[107] Ibid.

[108] *In re The Walt Disney Co Deriv Litig*, 825 A2d 275 (Del Ch 2003) ('Disney III').

[109] See discussion in section 3.1.3.

[110] Ibid (n 108).

[111] As the discussion above attests.

because the court was prevented—by the business judgment rule and the 102(b)(7) provision—from reaching it. The *Disney III* case suggested that knowing and deliberate indifference to a material corporate decision or potential risk of harm to the company may be satisfactory to conquer the DGCL 102(b)(7) provision.

This case left the company directors wondering whether every breach of duty of care claim could be pled as a failure to act in 'good faith'. It raised the question as to what does the concept of 'good faith' mean in practical application and what does it take to plead a claim for a lack of 'good faith' in relation to company directors' conduct? The Chancery Court's 2003 *Disney III* opinion, however, does not provide the answers to the above questions. The Court merged the issues of duty of loyalty and the duty of care together composing a picture of the company directors raising doubts in respect of their duty to act in 'good faith'.

3.3.2 *Official Comm. of Unsecured Creditors of Integrated Health Servs. Inc v Elkins, CA* No 20228-NC, 2004 Del Ch LEXIS 122 (Del Ch August 24, 2004)

In another 2004 Chancery Court case *Official Comm. of Unsecured Creditors of Integrated Health Servs. Inc v Elkins, CA* the plaintiff claimed that the company directors of Integrated Health Services had violated their fiduciary duties of care and loyalty when officially agreeing to some executive compensation and loan arrangements, mainly for the profit of the company chief executive officer, Elkins. Elkins benefited from a number of dubious compensation arrangements, including a large bonus, option grants and various loans.[112] Nevertheless, when the Chancery Court discovered that the compensation and loan arrangements had been officially

---

[112] *Official Comm of Unsecured Creditors of Integrated Health Servs Inc v Elkins CA* No 20228-NC 2004 Del Ch LEXIS 122, at 13–25 (Del Ch August 24, 2004).

agreed on by a majority of independent directors who had not been influenced by considerations of personal advantage, the court dismissed the plaintiff's allegations relating to the duty of loyalty.[113]

The Chancery Court analysed whether the challenged actions had been agreed on with an intentional and conscious disregard to the directors' duties upon which it was necessary to state a fiduciary duty of care claim which was not subject to exculpation as empowered by Section 102(b)(7) of the DGCL. From this perspective, the Chancery Court argued that, in discussing whether an action was taken with intentional and conscious disregard of directors' duties, it was necessary to determine whether the action is beyond unreasonable, and is in fact irrational. Therefore, the duty of care claim seemed to ask for dismissal. Nevertheless, the Chancery Court similarly to the *Disney III* case depended on the bad faith exclusion to Section 102(b)(7) of the DGCL in refusing to dismiss the claim.[114]

In its ruling the Chancery Court argued that, for the company director to act loyally, he/she needs to act in 'good faith' and in the belief that his/her actions are in the company's best interest; therefore, the duty of 'good faith' can be analysed as a part of the duty of loyalty. Furthermore, the duty of 'good faith' may be analysed as an element of the duty of care if the fault is a process failure, necessitating investigation of company directors' actions in respect of what the board did and did not do to stop the company from the loss.[115] As one can see from the above analysis, the court

---

[113] Delaware General Corporation Law (Title 8, Chapter 1 of the Delaware Code) § 144(a) (2001) is actually agreeing on a transaction involving a company and one of its directors if a majority of not influenced by considerations of personal advantage and independent directors having the knowledge of material facts regarding the involved director's interests agreed on the transaction.

[114] Ibid (n 133).

[115] Ibid 31-37.

suggested that the doctrine of 'good faith' has its elements in each of the traditional elements of fiduciary duty.

Therefore, the standards of good faith by the courts in *Disney III* and in *Unsecured Creditors of Integrated Health Services, Inc. v. Elkins* cases make it unclear as to what additional requirements may be determined to be subject to an intentional and conscious disregard that could constitute conduct in bad faith. Despite having a bunch of recent court cases and their decisions, the precise meaning of 'good faith' still remains an enigma and leaves this study with a question what is the essence of the duty of 'good faith'?

3.4 The Substance of Good Faith or the Language of Bad Faith

The duty of 'good faith' seems to drift between the meaning of duty of loyalty and the duty of care hence, as argued by former Chief Justice Veasey, 'the jurisprudence of 'good faith' [still remains] unresolved'[116] As a further attempt to study the substance of this doctrine the author turns to analysis of the language describing the conduct of bad faith used in the recent case law. As noticed by Griffith some of the cases recount the language of recklessness[117] and intentional disregard in characterizing conduct which is categorized as in bad faith.[118] As an example, the author

---

[116] EN Veasey, 'State-Federal Tension in Corporate Governance and the Professional Responsibilities of Advisors' (2003) 28 Journal of Corporation Law 441, 448.

[117] In criminal law, recklessness (also called unchariness) is one of the four possible classes of mental state constituting mens rea (the Latin for 'guilty mind'); F Stewart and L Mervyn, 'The Capacity for Recklessness' (1992) 12 (74) Legal Studies

[118] In criminal law, recklessness (also called unchariness) is one of the four possible classes of mental state constituting mens rea (the Latin

refocuses on the *Disney III* case where the court referred to the actions in bad-faith as 'knowing or deliberate indifference (...) to [the company director's] duty to act faithfully and with appropriate care is conduct (...) that may not have been taken honestly and in 'good faith' to advance the best interests of the company.'[119] In the *Elkins* case bad-faith has been described as 'intentional and conscious disregard to director's duties'[120] Sale takes this line of reasoning further and argues that 'good faith' concentrates on the aim, purpose or intent and that company directors failure to act in 'good faith' takes place 'when they [company directors] abdicate, subvert, or ignore [their] responsibilities, or act with deliberate indifference toward them.'[121] This conduct is deliberately indifferent, conspicuously bad, offensive, or insurgent and, according to her, requires 'motive based allegations of severely reckless or seemingly intentional behaviour'.[122] Sale suggests that acts of bad faith are 'severely reckless' acts.

The court in 2006 in the *David B Shaev Profit Sharing Account v Armstrong* company law case advances the understanding of good faith and holds that a good faith claim might lie if defendant directors 'wilfully or recklessly ignored information that would have to led to the discovery' of pervasive corporate misconduct'.[123] The court noted further that 'bad faith may be inferred where the board's decision is so far beyond the bounds of reasonableness

---

for 'guilty mind'); Griffith, SJ, 'Good Faith Business Judgment: A Theory of Rhetoric in Corporate Law Jurisprudence'(2005) 55(1) Duke Law Journal 29; See also, F Stewart and L Mervyn, 'The Capacity for Recklessness' (1992) 12 (74) Legal Studies 74.

[119] *In re Walt Disney Co Derivative Litig,* 825 A2d 275, 289 (Del Ch 2003).

[120] *Official Comm of Unsecured Creditors of Integrated Health Servs, Inc v Elkins,* CA No 20228-NC, 2004 Del Ch LEXIS 122 (2004).

[121] HA Sale, 'Delaware's Good Faith' (2004) 89 Cornell Law Review 456, 486.

[122] Ibid 488-89.

[123] *David B Shaev Profit Sharing Account v Armstrong CA* No 1449-N 2006 WL 391931 at 1* (Del Ch Feb 13 2006).

judgment that it seams essentially inexplicable on any other ground'[124]. Similarly, Veasey suggests that even though 'the concept of good faith is not fully developed in the case law, and factual scenarios are difficult to formulate, an argument could be made that reckless, disingenuous, irresponsible, or irrational conduct (...) could implicate concepts of good faith'[125].

The question then arises as to how to define the mental state of recklessness or deliberate indifference? Sale offers a solution to this concern and directs courts hearing company law cases with regard to the issues of reaching the duty of 'good faith' to follow the direction of *scienter* standard[126] of the federal securities law.[127] (It is necessary to make a small caveat here: Delaware courts have already utilized standards from federal securities law.)[128] *Scienter* is a main element of claims pursuant to section 10(b) of the 1934 Securities Exchange Act (hereafter referred to as 'the 1934 Act') [129]

---

[124] Ibid.

[125] EN Veasey, 'State-Federal Tension in Corporate Governance and the Professional Responsibilities of Advisors' (2003) 28 J Corp L 441, 447.

[126] In the United States, in order to prevail in a securities fraud claim under Section 10(b) of the Securities Exchange Act of 1934, a plaintiff must allege and prove that the defendant acted with *scienter*. The Private Securities Litigation Reform Act of 1995 added the requirement that a plaintiff must plead facts giving rise to a "strong inference" of *scienter*.

[127] Securities regulation in the United States is the part of USA law that takes into consideration various aspects of transactions and other dealings with securities. The term is usually understood to include both federal- and state-level regulation by purely governmental regulatory agencies. On the Federal level, the primary securities regulator is the Securities and Exchange Commission (SEC). State of Delaware follows the 1934 Securities Exchange Act on the federal level and the Delaware Uniform Securities Act on the state level.

[128] *Rosenblatt v Getty Oil Co*, 493 A2d 929 (1985).

[129] Securities Exchange Act of 1934, ch 404, 48 Stat 881 (codified as amended at 15 USC § 78j(b) (2000) <www.sec.gov/about/laws/sea34.pdf> accessed 17 August 2017.

and the accompanying Rule 10b-5[130]. In reviewing this element, courts focus on the defendants' state of mind in relation to the misstatement or omission.[131] Plaintiffs who want to succeed must plead *scienter*.[132] To comprehend the line of Sale's analysis, the next part of this discussion considers the 1934 Act with a special focus on the section 10(b) & 10b-5 and the concept of *scienter* with relation to the doctrine of 'good faith'.

---

[130] Ibid 10b-5.

[131] Ibid.

[132] *In re Westinghouse Sec Litig* 90 F3d 696, 707 (3d Cir 1996).

CHAPTER 4

RECKLESSNESS UNDER US COMMON LAW

4.1 1934 Securities Exchange Act Section 10(b) & 10b-5

The Securities Exchange Act of the United States was enacted in 1934. With this 1934 Act, the United States Congress created the US Securities and Exchange Commission[133] ('SEC'). The 1934 Act empowers the SEC with broad authority over all aspects of the securities industry. In this regard, the purpose of the 1934 Act is to provide for the regulation of securities exchanges and of over-the-counter markets operating in interstate and foreign commerce and through the mails. Furthermore, the aim of this 1934 Act is to prevent inequitable and unfair practices on such exchanges and markets.[134]

---

[133] The Securities and Exchange Commission oversees securities exchanges, securities brokers and dealers, investment advisors, and mutual funds in an effort to promote fair dealing, the disclosure of important market information, and to prevent fraud. <www.sec.gov> accessed 17 August 2017.

[134] Ibid.

Cross and Miller are of the opinion that Section 10(b) and Rule 10b-5[135] are the most important sections of the 1934 Act.[136] The former formally forbids the use of any manipulative or deceptive device which is in violation of SEC rules and regulations. The latter prohibits any acts or omissions resulting in fraud or deceit in connection with the purchase or sale of any security. For the SEC Rule 10b-5 to be invoked, there must be intentional fraud or deceit by the party charged with the violation. Fraud can also happen through reckless conduct. In order to establish a claim under the SEC Rule 10b-5 plaintiffs (including the SEC) is obliged to show (a) Manipulation or deception (through misrepresentation and/or omission); (b) Materiality; (c) 'In Connection With' the purchase or sale of securities; and (d) *Scienter.*[137]

---

[135] Ibid (n 138) 'Rule 10b-5: Employment of Manipulative and Deceptive Practices': 'It shall be unlawful for any person, directly or indirectly, by the use of any means or instrumentality of interstate commerce, or of the mails or of any facility of any national securities exchange; (a) To employ any device, scheme, or artifice to defraud, (b) To make any untrue statement of a material fact or to omit to state a material fact necessary in order to make the statements made, in the light of the circumstances under which they were made, not misleading, or (c) To engage in any act, practice, or course of business which operates or would operate as a fraud or deceit upon any person, in connection with the purchase or sale of any security'.

[136] F Cross and R Miller, *The Legal Environment of Business: Text and Cases -- Ethical, Regulatory, Global, and E-Commerce Issues* (Cengage Learning 2008) 688.

[137] Securities Exchange Act of 1934, Rule 10b-5.

4.1.1 *Scienter* Standard and Recklessness under Case Law

The recklessness standard has been applied by many federal courts as an appropriate *scienter* requirement for fraud claims, albeit in other contexts.[138]

One of the first times in law the *scienter* standard, however, was taken into consideration is the 1976 securities law case of *Ernest & Ernest v. Hochfielder*.[139] It was a United States Supreme Court case which addressed whether proof of violation of a 10b-5 claim should require *scienter* or maybe something less.[140] The Court held that the language and the history of the statute demanded something more than negligence or a failure to perform an act that is required by law and, in fact, allowed liability only for people who fail to act in 'good faith'.[141] Here, the court drew the line between 'good faith' and bad faith as one of the ways in which it restricted recklessness.[142]

---

[138] *Ottmann v Hanger Orthopedic Grp Inc* 353 F3d 338, 343 (4th Cir 2003) (citing various circuits' adoptions of recklessness as scienter for securities fraud).

[139] *Ernst & Ernst v Hochfelder* 425 US 185 (1976). Also the federal Courts of Appeal generally agree that recklessness suffices as a form of *scienter*. See, for example, *Hoffman v Estabrook & Co* 587 F 2d 509, 516 (1st Cir 1978); *Rolf v Blyth, Eastman Dillon & Co* 570 F 2d 38, 44-47 (2d Cir) *cert denied* 439 US 1039 (1978); *Coleco Indus Inc v Berman* 567 F 2d 569, 574 (3rd Cir 1977) *cert denied* 439 US 830 (1978); *First Va Bankshares v Benson* 559 F 2d 1307, 1314 (5th Cir 1977) *cert denied* 435 US 952 (1978).

[140] The Supreme Court of the United States was established pursuant to Article III of the United States Constitution in 1789 as the highest federal court in the United States. It has ultimate appellate jurisdiction over all federal courts and over state court cases involving issues of federal law, and original jurisdiction over a small range of cases <www.supremecourt.gov> accessed 17 August 2017.

[141] *Ernst & Ernst v Hochfelder* at 206.

[142] *Ernst & Ernst v Hochfelder* at 205.

The case of *Ernest & Ernest* provided information on what amounts to reckless or scandalous behaviour in the respect of *scienter*. The case drew a line based on a connection between the defendants' knowledge and their misstatements or omissions. *Scienter* need not necessarily be pleaded with facts which suggest actual knowledge. For example, in the 1976 securities law case of *Franke v. Midwestern* it was held that in notably egregious behaviour, it is presumed that knowledge of an omission or misstatement existed, or should have existed.[143]

There are more recent cases where the courts determine that *scienter* requirement could be satisfied upon a showing of 'recklessness.' In a 2001- case involving a securities fraud claim, namely *Matrixx Initiatives Inc v Siracusano* the Supreme Court assumed that the *scienter* requirement can be met upon proving 'deliberate recklessness'.[144] The Court ascertained that ''a reasonable person" would deem the inference that (petitioner) acted with deliberate recklessness (...) at least as compelling as any opposing inference.'[145] Furthermore, in the 2011 security fraud case *In re J.P. Jeanneret Assocs Inc* the court also held that '[a] "strong inference" of scienter can be established through factual allegations showing "motive and opportunity to commit fraud' or 'strong circumstantial evidence of conscious misbehavior or recklessness."'[146] This just raises a further question, namely: what is *recklessness*?

---

[143] *Franke v Midwestern Okla Dev Auth* 428 F Supp 719 (WD Okla 1976) The court defined reckless conduct as follows: 'reckless conduct may be defined as a highly unreasonable omission, involving not merely simple, or even inexcusable negligence, but an extreme departure from the standards of ordinary care, and which presents a danger of misleading buyers or sellers that is either known to the defendant or is so obvious that the actor must have been aware of it.'

[144] *Matrixx Initiatives Inc v Siracusano* 131 S Ct 1309, 1323–24 (2011).

[145] Ibid 1325.

[146] *In re JP Jeanneret Assocs Inc* 769 F Supp 2d 340, 354 (SDNY 2011) (quoting *In re AOL Time Warner Inc & ERISA Litig* 381 F Supp 2d 192,

4.2 Recklessness at Federal Securities Law from the perspective of Common Law

In the 1978 securities law case of *Roolf v Blyth, Eastman Dillon & Co. INC* the court held '[It] is unquestionable that the common law has served as an interpretive source of securities law concepts'.[147] This study follows this argument when defining the standard of recklessness and turns to the common law for its definition. As suggested by Vetri '[r]ecklessness is a more culpable type of fault than negligence and usually can be invoked in accident situations where the conduct shows a conscious disregard of a high risk of harm. Recklessness falls somewhere between intentional misconduct and negligence on the culpability continuum.'[148] Put differently, at common law recklessness is interpreted as a concept finding its place between intentional conduct on one extreme and negligence at the other.[149] Hence, as noted by Rapp '"[r]ecklessness" is one of the oldest concepts in Anglo-American tort law, and it is also one of the most poorly understood.'[150]

The degree of culpability in each of these concepts from the perspective of intentionality, risk and harm differ in terms of mental culpability.[151] In the 1964 securities law case of *United States v. Benjamin* the court held that it is strongly probable that the

---

218 (SDNY 2004)).

[147] *Roolf v Blyth, Eastman Dillon & Co* INC 570 F2d 38, 45 (1978) quoting *Holdsworth v Strong* 545 F 2d 687, 693-95 (10th Cir 1976).

[148] D Vetri et al, *Tort Law and Practice* (5th edn, Carolina Academic Press 2016) 17.

[149] P Keeton, 'Fraud: The Necessity for an Intent to Deceive' (1965) 5 University of California at Los Angeles Law Review 583; JP Bolger, 'Recklessness and the Rule 10b-5 Scienter Standard after Hochfelder' (1981) 49 Fordham L Rev 817.

[150] GC Rapp, 'The Wreckage of Recklessness' (2008) 86 Wash U L REV 111, 111.

[151] H Gross, *A Theory of Criminal Justice* (Oxford University Press 1979) 77-82.

reckless act will result in harm, even though the reckless actor was acting in disregard of that risk.[152] In light of the probability of future harm, recklessness has been described as a form of knowing conduct.[153] In the 1976 drug trafficking case of *United States v. Jewell* the court stated that 'knowingly in (...) statutes is not limited to positive knowledge, but includes the state of mind of one who does not possess positive knowledge only because he consciously avoided it.'[154] Hart asserts that the reckless actor does not possess actual knowledge because he/she is not conscious of the existence of a fact that can be proved by subjective evidence.[155] As an outcome the difference between these two mental states can be drawn by a picture of a reckless actor who 'should have known that his/her conduct was fraudulent[156] and the knowing actor who 'must have known' of the risk of harm to plaintiff(s) that would result from his/her action.[157]

Furthermore, courts have generally identified that the wilfulness existing essentially in a knowledgeable act also has its place in reckless conduct.[158] As an example, we may take into consideration was the 1964 securities law case of *United States v. Benjamin* where an accountant made as a matter of a form a financial statement and fraudulently sold unregistered securities, failing to investigate the providing corporation's accounts, and

---

[152] *United States v Benjamin* 328 F2d 854, 861-63 (2d Cir 1964); Restatement (Second) of Torts § 500 (1977).

[153] *Rochez Bros Inc v Rhoades* 491 F2d 402, 407 & n6 (3d Cir 1974).

[154] *United States v Jewell* 532 F2d 697, 702 (1976).

[155] HAL Hart, *Punishment and Responsibility Essays in the Philosophy of the Law* (Clarendon Press 1975) 152.

[156] See, for example, *Stern v American Bankshares Corp* 429 F Supp 818, 826 (ED Wis 1977); *SEC v Coven* 581 F 2d 1020, 1028 (2d Cir 1978) cert denied 440 US 950 (1979).

[157] See, for example, *Sanders v John Nuveen & Co* 554 F2d 790, 793 (7th Cir 1977); *McLean v Alexander* 599 F2d 1190, 1198 (3d Cir 1979).

[158] JP Bolger, 'Recklessness and the Rule 10b-5 Scienter Standard after Hochfelder' (1980) 49(5) Fordham Law Review 824.

incorporated non-existing assets.[159] In order to establish whether there was enough supporting evidence to demonstrate that the defendant had the required degree of mental degree of mental culpability, the court acknowledged the difference between actual and imputed knowledge and stated that the wilfulness involved is the same.[160] The court held that, while there is no permissible conclusion of knowledge from the fact itself of insincerity, there are many cases where, from the defendant's special situation and continuity of conduct, an indication that the defendant knew the insincerity of what he did may lawfully be drawn.[161] It has been stated that in this type of situation the defendant is reckless because he 'deliberately close[s] his eyes to facts he ha[s] a duty to see'[162] and as a consequence is considered guilty of conscious fraud.

Interestingly for this research, the US Court of Appeals for the Third Circuit, a federal court with appellate jurisdiction over the district courts of Delaware, in the 2010 criminal tax case of *United States v. Stadtmauer* held that 'wilful blindness' requires an element of knowledge, which would be satisfied if it is proved that 'the defendant closed his eyes to what would otherwise have been obvious to the defendant. (...) Stated another way, the defendant's knowledge of a fact or circumstance may be inferred from his wilful blindness to the existence of that fact and circumstance.'[163] The Third Circuit found that, generally, to act 'knowingly' means to act with an awareness of the high probability of the existence of a fact. When such an awareness is present, 'positive' knowledge is not required. The Court held that a similarly worded instruction would equate 'wilful blindness' with reckless disregard.[164]

---

[159] *United States v Benjamin* 328 F2d 854, 861-63 (2d Cir 1964).
[160] Ibid 862-863.
[161] Ibid 861 – 862.
[162] Ibid 862.
[163] *United States v Stadtmauer* 620 F3d 238, 253 (3rd Cir 2010).
[164] Ibid.

This is not to say that courts will or should apply recklessness that would equate with 'wilful blindness' as a *scienter* requirement for directors' breach of the duty to act in 'good faith' in the best interests of the company. The author recognises that for these types of claims, courts will be required to agree on the meaning of recklessness and whether or not this particular standard should be employed. It is interesting to recognise, however, on the basis of the courts determinations that 'wilful blindness' might be found with showing of objective of recklessness.

In light of the above, the discussion begins with an analogy from the doctrine of 'wilful blindness', borrowed from criminal law, but which has recently been used in federal security law cases.[165] The author argues that the recklessness standard shares similarities with the doctrine of 'wilful blindness' and as such might share similarities with company directors falling foul of the duty to act in 'good faith' in the best interests of the company. Consequently, further research will focus on whether it would be appropriate to cross-apply the doctrines of 'good faith' and 'wilful blindness' as suggested at the beginning of this analysis. Before taking the next step a short analysis of the state of mind, including the level of *scienter*, which is required by the criminal and civil prosecution, will take place.

4.3 State of Mind - Level of *Scienter* of Company Directors under Federal Securities Law

Whether a person is liable for a certain type of action generally depends on the personal level of involvement in the conduct and the person's state of mind, or *scienter*, at the particular time when the

---

[165] *United States v Ebbers* 458 F3d 110, 124 (2d Cir 2006); *SEC v Jerome Krantz, Cary Chasin, and Gary Nadelman*, Civil Action No 0:11-cv-60432-WPD (US District Court for the Southern District of Florida, filed February 28, 2011).

particular conduct took place.[166] In Hurt's view, criminal prosecutions required some proof of a higher level of *scienter* on the part of the defendant in the past; otherwise, civil action would be required. For example, most of the criminal laws 'require some degree of at least recklessness, if not intention'.[167]Krawiec suggests that prosecutors involved in criminal prosecutions of company directors have difficulty in proving that a high-ranking individual had actual knowledge of the company's misconduct. Or more precisely, they find it difficult to prove that the defendant (company director) was directing the misconduct[168] and as indicated by Stout, the determination of the motion to dismiss stage in a civil lawsuit could be 'determined at least as much by what the judge had for breakfast.'[169]

However, Charlow noticed that in recent civil prosecutions, the government was lawfully proceeding under a 'conscious avoidance' or wilful ignorance doctrine of criminal liability.[170] The prosecution may submit the theory that the defendant is guilty of securities fraud, if (a) there was an element of knowledge in this dispute and (b) the defendant was found to be in the position of being aware of a high probability of the fact in dispute and wilfully avoided confirming this fact.[171] For example, in the 2006 securities law case

---

[166] C Hurt, 'The Undercivilization of Corporate Law' (2007) U Illinois Law & Economics Research Paper No LE07-005, 413 <http://ssrn.com/abstract=965871 or <http://dx. doi.org/10.2139/ssrn.965871> accessed 17 August 2017.

[167] Ibid.

[168] KD Krawiec, 'Corporate Decisionmaking: Organizational Misconduct: Beyond the Principal-Agent Model' (2005) 32 Florida State University Law Review 571.

[169] LA Stout, 'Type I Error, Type II Error, and the Private Securities Litigation Reform Act' (1996) 38 Arizona Law Review 711, 712.

[170] R Charlow, 'Willful Ignorance and Criminal Culpability' (1992) 70 Texas Law Review 1351.

[171] *United States v Rodriguez* 983 F2d 455, 458 (2d Cir1993); See generally *United States v Civelli* 883 F2d 191, 194-95 (2d Cir), cert denied, 493 US 966, 110 S Ct 409, 107 L Ed 2d 374 (1989).

of *United States v. Ebbers* under the theory of 'wilful blindness' or conscious avoidance, Bernard Ebbers (CEO of WorldCom), was charged with one count of securities fraud and seven counts of making false filings with the SEC in the absence of knowledge of the specific illegal acts.[172]

The *United States v. Ebbers* case refers this study back to the idea of recklessness as discussed in the 1964 securities law case of *United States v. Benjamin,*[173] where the court held that the defendant was reckless because he 'deliberately closed his eyes to facts he had a duty to see'[174] and was consequently considered guilty of conscious fraud. The defendant wilfully closing his eyes to the facts which he/she should have noticed has been described by some scholars as conscious avoidance which is a doctrine that redefines one's knowledge to include conscious disregard of facts that are highly likely to exist.[175]

---

[172] *United States v Ebbers* 458 F3d 110, 124 (2d Cir 2006).

[173] *United States v Benjamin* 328 F2d 854, 861-63 (2d Cir 1964).

[174] Ibid 862.

[175] AD Lowell and KC Arnold, 'Corporate Crime after 2000: A New Law Enforcement Challenge or Deja Vu' (2003) 40 American Criminal Law Review 219, 230.

CHAPTER 5

WILFUL BLINDNESS IN DELAWARE

5.1 Wilful Blindness in Delaware

The 'wilful blindness' doctrine has been generally interpreted as being equivalent to knowledge.[176] As observed by Williams: 'The rule that "wilful blindness" is equivalent to knowledge is essential, and is found throughout the criminal law. It is, at the same time, an unstable rule, because judges are apt to forget its very limited scope.'[177] Williams continues:

> 'A court can properly find wilful blindness only where it can almost be said that the defendant actually knew. He suspected the fact; he realised its probability; but he refrained from obtaining the final confirmation because he wanted in the event to be able to deny knowledge. This, and this alone, is wilful blindness. It requires in effect a

---

[176] K Heller and M Dubber, *The Handbook of Comparative Criminal Law* (Stanford University Press 2010) 108.

[177] G Williams, *Criminal Law. The General Part* (2nd edn, Sweet & Maxwell 1961) 159.

finding that the defendant intended to cheat the administration of justice. Any wider definition would make the doctrine of "wilful blindness" indistinguishable from the civil doctrine of negligence in not obtaining knowledge. [178]

Hence, 'wilful blindness' doctrine could be applied to a conduct of a person (e.g. company director) who has become aware of the need for some more inquiry and declines to make this enquiry because he/she did not wish to face the consequences of the truth.

As suggested by Lowell and Arnold the doctrine has its origin in drug trafficking cases.[179] Since then it has been extended to different types of prosecution and is increasingly used in cases of company directors' securities fraud.[180] The SEC has applied this doctrine in a recent civil enforcement case of *SEC v Jerome Krantz, Cary Chasin and Gary Nadelman* in February 2011, when it sued three former directors of DHB Industries, alleging that they were 'wilfully blind to numerous red flags signalling accounting fraud' that enabled the former CEO to 'steal some ten million American dollars from DHB.'[181]

In the 2011 civil patent infringement case of *Global-Tech Appliances, Inc. v. SEB S.A.*[182] the Supreme Court affirmed the validity of this doctrine in both civil and criminal settings, but also established some standards for its application beyond those required in most federal circuit courts. This was noted in the dissent: 'the

---

[178] Ibid.

[179] AD Lowell and KC Arnold (n 175) see *United States v Jewell* 532 F2d 697 (1976).

[180] *SEC v Jerome Krantz, Cary Chasin and Gary Nadelman*, filed February 28, 2011 <www.sec.gov/litigation/complaints/2011/comp21867-directors.pdf> accessed 17 August 2017.

[181] *SEC v Krantz* et al, case 0:11-cv-60432 [SD Fla].

[182] *Global-Tech Appliances Inc et al v SEB SA*, No 10-6 (US May 31, 2011).

Court appears to endorse the 'wilful blindness' doctrine here for all federal criminal cases involving knowledge.'[183] As argued by Ball, the reason why the court applied 'wilful blindness' in this civil case was that circuit courts have overwhelmingly 'applied the doctrine to a wide range of criminal statutes.'[184] How then should an application of 'wilful blindness' proceed?

A good start is to discuss the background to the notion of 'wilful blindness' from the perspective of different criminal scenarios. In order to do so, this study will explore the historical development of 'wilful blindness'. It will analyse the doctrine of wilful blindness from the perspective of the case law of the United States Court of Appeals for the Third Circuit which is a federal court with appellate jurisdiction over the district of Delaware. Finally, this study will take the doctrine of 'wilful blindness' into consideration from the perspective of company directors' criminal liability in Delaware, and will discuss how this debate can be mapped onto the concept of recklessness and the doctrine of 'good faith'.

5.2 Historical Development of Wilful Blindness in Criminal Law

The doctrine of 'wilful blindness' has its roots in 19th century England. In the 1861 criminal law case of *Regina v. Sleep,* the court held that the defendant could be guilty of being in possession of 'naval stores' only if there was evidence that he either knew that the goods were owned by the government or if he 'wilfully shut his eyes

---

[183] Ibid 10.

[184] Ibid at 8 and DC Ball, Improving 'Willful Blindness' Jury Instructions in Criminal Cases After High Court's Decision in Global-Tech <http://lawprofessors.typepad.com/files/bnainsights.ball2.pdf> accessed 17 August 2017.

to the fact'.[185] In 1899, for the first time in US history the federal courts acknowledged the existence of the 'wilful blindness' doctrine in US law. This was in the false pretences[186] case of *Spurr v. United States* when the Court of Appeal held that the bank officer, who was convicted of certifying a check when he was aware of the fact that the drawer was lacking funds, was guilty of 'evil design'.[187] The verdict of 'evil design' was understood as purposely keeping himself in ignorance as to whether the drawer had sufficient funds in the account or not.[188] The court took into consideration the priority of 'wilful blindness' as an alternative to the statutory *mens rea*[189] requirement.

The doctrine gains momentum in the 1970s when there was a growing number of prosecutions for illegal drugs in the US.[190] For example, *United States v. Jewell* was a federal case that mentioned deliberate ignorance. The defendant Jewell was excused and convicted of importing marijuana in his vehicle while driving from Mexico to the US.[191] In court, when he was requested to offer his

---

185 *Regina v Sleep* 169 Rev Rep 1296 (QB 1861).

186 False pretences, or more properly called 'obtaining property by false pretences', is a crime where someone lies or makes misrepresentations in order to obtain someone else's property. As argued by Fletcher United States statutes on this subject are mainly copied from the English statutes, and the courts there in a general way follow the English interpretations; GP Fletcher, *Rethinking Criminal Law* (Oxford University Press 2000) 10.

187 *Spurr v United States* 174 US 728 (1899).

188 Ibid 734.

189 'Mens rea is defined as the culpable state of mind that a defendant must have in concurrence with the act in order to commit the prohibited criminal conduct.' J Delaney, *How to Do Your Best on Law School Exams* (John Delaney Publications 1988) 39.

190 KL Chesnut, 'Comment, U.S. v. Alvaredo: Reflections on a Jewell' (1989) 19 Golden Gate University Law Review 47, 49.

191 *United States v Jewell* 532 US 697 (en banc), cert denied, 426 US 951 (1976).

version of the story the defendant testified that he was unaware of what had been in his vehicle. After this trial, the Court agreed on an instruction that the jury could convict Jewell if it found that the defendant was unaware of the illegal drugs which he had in his vehicle as long as the defendant's ignorance was exclusively a result of him having made 'a conscious purpose to disregard that which was in his vehicle'[192]

5.3 Wilful Blindness under the United States Court of Appeals for the Third Circuit Case Law

Most recently, in the 2013 drug trafficking case of *United States v. Caraballo-Rodriguez*[193] Richard Caraballo-Rodriguez was convicted of transporting a controlled substance, namely cocaine, from San Juan, Puerto Rico, to Philadelphia, Pennsylvania. The evidence only showed that the defendant knew that he was being entrusted with a large suitcase which might have contained different items including stolen jewellery, laundered money, stolen computer chips, and counterfeiting plates.[194] A jury held that the government could meet the expectations of the 'knowledge' condition by clearly showing the existence of actual knowledge or 'reckless disregard'[195]. The wilful blindness has been described by the court further as 'a subjective state of mind that is deemed to satisfy a *scienter* requirement of knowledge.'[196] The Third Circuit has also held that, if supported by the evidence, it is not uncommon for a court to give instructions on both actual knowledge and wilful blindness,

---

[192] Ibid at 700.
[193] *United States v Caraballo-Rodriguez* 786 F3d 418, 420 fn2 (3d Cir 2013).
[194] Ibid.
[195] Ibid 4.
[196] Supp App 44 (quoting *United States v Idowu*, 157 F3d 265, 268 (3d Cir 1998).

because if the jury does not find actual knowledge, it might still find wilful blindness.[197]

Among the Third Circuit cases that show the situations in which a verdict of wilful blindness was given to the company director was the 2005 case of *United States v. Brodie*.[198] The company director was convicted of conspiracy to violate the Trading with the Enemy Act (1917)[199] and Cuban Assets Control Regulations[200]. The court required proof that the company director knew the facts that gave legal grounds to the offence and that the defendant knew the lawful purpose of the conspiracy. In addition, the court required that the defendant knew the law prohibiting his conduct and that he acted with the specific intent to circumvent that law. When the defendant was interrogated, he denied having that knowledge or intent. He insisted that he had asserted that his presumption was that the transactions in question were being handled lawfully through Canadian and United Kingdom companies, not unlawfully through a United States company.

---

[197] See the Third Circuit's Model Criminal Jury Instructions available at <www.ca3.uscourts.gov/modeljuryinstructions.htm> accessed 17 August 2017. See also *United States v One 1973 Rolls Royce* 43 F 3d 794, 807-08 (3d Cir 1994).

[198] *United States v Brodie* case 403 F3d 123 (3d Cir 2005).

[199] The Trading with the Enemy Act of 1917 (40 Stat 411, enacted 6 October 1917, codified at 12 USC § 95a et seq), sometimes abbreviated as TWEA, is a United States federal law to restrict trade with countries hostile to the United States <www.treasury.gov/resource-center/sanctions/Documents/twea.pdf> accessed 17 August 2017.

[200] The Cuban Assets Control Regulations, 31 CFR 515, are regulations of the United States Department of the Treasury on July 8, 1963, under the Trading with the Enemy Act of 1917, that general regulate relations between Cuba and the U.S. and are the main mechanism of domestic enforcement of the United States embargo against Cuba <www.ecfr.gov/cgibin/textidx?SID=12a5297a732bf340226764fa64ac6f23&node=31:3.1.1.1.4&rgn=div5> accessed 17 August 2017.

Evidence showed that the defendant recognized the likelihood that the United States entity was involved in illegal transactions with Cuba yet, as stated by the court the defendant 'deliberately avoided learning the true facts'[201]. This included evidence suggesting that the defendant tried to ensure that he never saw a direct reference to Cuba, that the corporate culture was to refer to Cuba by 'code words,'[202] that the defendant failed to ask the 'natural follow-up question(s),'[203] and that the defendant never instigated any follow-ups to his own instructions to ensure that his company was not transacting business with Cuba.[204] The Third Circuit held that the trial judge properly instructed the jury on 'wilful blindness'.

The announcements of the US Court of Appeal for the Third Circuit take the position that the mental state requirement of 'wilful blindness' has been met if there is an aspect of awareness of the pertinent facts or circumstances that amount to crime therefore reckless conduct of the defendant. A similar position has been presented by the Model Penal Code and will be shortly explained in the next part of this study.

5.4 Wilful Blindness from the Perspective of Company Directors' Criminal Liability in Delaware

Under the US Constitution, the power to impose criminal liability is reserved primarily for the states, with federal authority limited to the prohibition and punishment of crimes related to federal interests (e.g. federal securities).[205] As indicated by Robinson the

---

[201] *United States v Brodie* case 403 F3d 123 (3d Cir 2005).

[202] Ibid 35.

[203] Ibid 77.

[204] Ibid 133.

[205] PH Robinson, 'The American Model Penal Code: A Brief Overview' (2007) 10 New Criminal Law Review 319.

Model Penal Code (MPC), more than any other code, is the closest thing to being an American criminal code.[206] It creates legal grounds for the State of Delaware and its company directors' criminal liability this include the interpretation of the doctrine of 'wilful blindness'.[207]

5.5 Wilful Blindness under the Model Penal Code

'Requirement of Knowledge Satisfied by Knowledge of High Probability. When knowledge of the existence of a particular fact is an element of an offense, such knowledge is established if a person is aware of a high probability of its existence, unless he actually believes that it does not exist.'[208]

Designers of the MPC developed the concept of 'wilful blindness' by first generally defining 'knowledge' in relation to the essence of the defendant's (e.g. company director) behaviour.[209] The defendant who committed the act, even though he/she knew that it was highly probable that a specific fact took place, is just as culpable as the defendant who had a 'virtually certain knowledge.'[210] The defendant must only be aware that his/her conduct was of the nature that caused particular results[211] and as suggested by Marcus

---

[206] Ibid.

[207] RS Gruner, *Corporate Criminal Liability and Prevention* (Law Journal Press 2004) 40.

[208] Model Penal Code, 2.02 General Requirements of Culpability (7).

[209] DN Husak and CA Callender, 'Wilful Ignorance, Knowledge, and the 'Equal Culpability' Thesis: A Study of the Deeper Significance of the Principles of Legality' (1994) Wisconsin Law Review 29, 36.

[210] JL Marcus, 'Model Penal Code Section 2.02(7) and Willful Blindness' (1993) 102(8) The Yale Law Journal 2235-36.

[211] Model Penal Code (n 208).

the best justification for a wilful ignorance charge is the defendant's lack of concern with regard to the existence of crime itself.[212] Luban notices further that draftsmen of the MPC accepted a state of high awareness of the nature of the element of the crime would make defendants equally culpable with those defendants who acted with full awareness of their behaviour, its circumstances and the results of their actions.[213]

For Edwards this state of mind 'has generally been described as connivance or constructive knowledge, and approximates closely to the concept of recklessness'.[214] Robbins notes that the 'high-probability language of the Code [MPC section 2.02(7)] indicates recklessness.'[215] In addition, Buell argues that the most precise and demanding definition of recklessness, and the one that is most often used in criminal law, is that which is found in the MPC: the conscious disregard of a substantial and unjustifiable risk - provided that the actor's disregard of that risk grossly deviates from how a reasonable person would act in the same circumstances.[216] Under this definition, recklessness is a form of 'knowledge'. The actor is actually aware of the risk that is inherent in the situation, as opposed to, in the case of a full knowledge requirement, having the practical certainty that it inheres. The author supports Edwards and Buell in calling this the conscious-disregard, wilful blindness, or wilful ignorance form of recklessness.[217]

Clearly, a close affinity exists between wilful blindness and the state of mind described as recklessness. It envisages the mind of a

---

[212] JL Marcus (n 210) 2235-36.

[213] D Luban, 'Contrived Ignorance' (1999) 87 Georgia Law Journal 961-965.

[214] J Edwards, 'The Criminal Degrees of Knowledge' (1954) 17 Modern Law Review 294, 298.

[215] I Robbins, 'The Ostrich Instruction: Deliberate Ignorance as a Criminal Mens Rea' (1990) 81 Journal of Criminal Law and Criminology 223.

[216] S Buell, 'In What Is Securities Fraud?' (2011) 61 Duke Law Journal 511, 534-36.

[217] Ibid.

person who actually foresees the consequences of his/her actions and even though not seeking those consequences, deliberately takes the risk of their happening. Hence, 'take whichever definition of connivance you please - in particular, the wilful shutting of the eyes to obvious means of knowledge - and the close relationship which exists between the two concepts [recklessness and 'wilful blindness'] becomes immediately evident'.[218]

5.6 Comparing Definitions of Wilful Ignorance with Knowledge and Recklessness in Relation to Company Directors' Bad Faith

The author favours the opinion that the doctrine of 'wilful blindness' could be cross-applied with recklessness. This in turn, due to the argumentation provided by Sale, could serve as an interpretative source of acts of company directors falling foul of the duty to act in 'good faith'. Wilful blindness, as drafted by the MPC, requires a connection between recklessness and knowledge. Recklessness and knowledge, as defined by the MPC, differ in terms of the awareness of the important facts in question. Wilful ignorance, as well as recklessness and knowledge, demands that the defendant is subjectively aware of a 'high probability' of the fact in question.[219] Quinton argues that the defendant (e.g. company director) 'knows' when he/she is aware of the firm conviction that something is the case, or almost or nearly aware of the firm conviction that something is the case.[220] However, in order for the defendant (e.g. company director) to be reckless, meaning to act in bad faith, he/she must be aware of, at most, the

---

[218] J Edwards, 'The Criminal Degrees of Knowledge' (1954) 17 Modern Law Review 294, 304.

[219] Model Penal Code (n 208).

[220] AM Quinton, *Knowledge and Belief, in The Encyclopedia of Philosophy*, Volume 4, 346.

substantial probability of a fact in question.[221] Charlow suggests that the awareness of the defendant (e.g. company director), who is aware of the high probability of the fact in question, takes its place somewhere between the level of conviction demanded for knowledge and the one demanded for recklessness.[222]

Wilful blindness falls more in the frames of recklessness than in knowledge. In order for the defendant (e.g. company director) to be charged with recklessness, he/she must be aware of the substantiality of the risk he/she faces, or factors making the risk substantial, which is the MPC-based description of wilful blindness. Furthermore, like recklessness and unlike knowledge, the MPC formulation of wilful blindness does not require a belief about the fact in question. The reckless defendant (e.g. company director) may disregard his/her awareness of the probability of a fact in question without deciding whether or not he/she personally believes it to exist. Likewise, as long as the wilfully ignorant defendant (e.g. company director) is aware of the high probability of a fact, he/she may act despite that fact without formulating a personal opinion as to whether or not it exists. This is not so for the defendant who knows the fact, because this knowledge requires belief.

The author offers an example to demonstrate that the wilfully blind company director is not necessarily a knowing actor and therefore a reckless actor[223], and, consequently, a bad-faith actor.

---

[221] R Charlow, 'Willful Ignorance and Criminal Culpability' (1992) 70 Texas Law Review 1382.

[222] Ibid.

[223] In the 1978 securities law case of *Roolf v Blyth, Eastman Dillon & Co INC* 570 F2d 38, 45 (1978) the court held '[It] is unquestionable that the common law has served as an interpretive source of securities law concepts'. Consequently, Buell favours the opinion that most precise and demanding definition of recklessness, and the one most often used in law, is the one found in the MPC: the conscious disregard of a substantial and unjustifiable risk - provided that the actor's disregard of

First hypothetical scenario: *When a wilfully blind company director is not necessarily a knowing actor and therefore a reckless actor and, consequently, a bad-faith actor.*

Two directors of a Diamond Jewellery company, A and B, both of whom have exactly the same amount of information with respect to the proposition that one particular gemstone is a diamond. Both think there is a reasonable chance that the gem is a diamond but they are not sure. Although this is theoretically possible, in reality it may not actually be the case. They could consult a jeweller but lets us assume that there is no jeweller available. Without their actual knowledge, we as observers know that the gem is in fact a diamond. Suppose further that the company director A lacks this knowledge. Finally, let us assume that there is nothing more which he can reasonably do to investigate the matter further.

Accordingly, company director A is 'non-wilfully ignorant'. In contrast, company director B is different from company director A, only in that he has an additional method of investigation open to him: he knows that only a diamond can scratch a ruby, and he happens to have a ruby in his possession. For whatever reason, he consciously decides not to employ this test. Accordingly, he remains wilfully ignorant, furthermore reckless and therefore acting in bad faith because of his conscious disregard of a substantial and unjustifiable risk whether the gem is in fact a diamond or not. As both company directors A and B have the same amount of information and both see it as equally likely that the gem is a diamond, but company director A lacks knowledge, we can conclude that company director B also lacks knowledge. Thus, B is a wilfully ignorant and reckless, and therefore can be seen as an individual who lacks knowledge and acts in bad-faith.

---

that risk grossly deviates from how a reasonable person would act in the same circumstances. S Buell, 'In What Is Securities Fraud?' (2011) 61 Duke Law Journal 511, 534-36.

PART III

ENGLAND, UK

CHAPTER 6

COMPANY DIRECTORS' DUTY OF GOOD FAITH UNDER ENGLISH LAW

6.1 Good Faith under English Law

The New Oxford English Dictionary defines the term 'good faith' as 'honest or sincerity of intention.'[224] Some legal scholars, such as O'Connor suggests further that there are recurring themes in case law that take into consideration this expression widening its meaning to 'fairness'.[225] As such, 'good faith' is required in a wide range of situations, including contracts and business dealings, as well as during mediation, arbitration, or settlement negotiations in personal injury or similar tort cases.[226] It is not surprising then that the obligation to act in 'good faith' is an important element of English company law. As required by English law, the company

---

[224] J Pearsall (ed), *New Oxford Dictionary of English* (Oxford University Press 2001) 790.

[225] J O'Connor, *Good Faith in English Law* (Dartmouth Publishing 1990) 99-102.

[226] J De Lacy, *Reform of UK Company Law* (Routledge 2013).

directors are obligated by their fiduciary duties to act in 'good faith' when dealing on behalf of the company.[227] The next part of this analysis will focus on the development of the duty of 'good faith' under the pre-existing English common law position. Subsequently, this research will take into consideration section 309(1) of the Companies Act 1985 ('the Act 1985')[228] and will analyse the historical development of the *bona fide* (in 'good faith') rule from the perspective of English case law. This will further lead to an analysis of the company directors' duty of 'good faith' under the Companies Act 2006 ('the Act 2006')[229].

6.1.1 Law Governing the Company Directors' Fiduciary Duty of Good Faith before the Companies Act 2006

Keay argues that the duty to act *bona fide* in the best interests of the company has been a part of UK company law since the mid-19 century.[230] Before the 2006 Act was established in English law, company directors' fiduciary duties were composed of regulatory and self-regulatory mechanisms.[231] For Sheikh, the regulatory mechanisms that were supposed to ensure that company directors acted within their duties have been represented mainly by fiduciary duties, the common law duty and statutory duties which were imposed on directors under legislation such as the Companies Act

---

227 Companies Act (2006) s 172(1) <www.legislation.gov.uk/ukpga/2006/46/section/172> accessed 17 August 2017.

228 The Companies Act 1985 section 309(1) <www.legislation.gov.uk/ukpga/1985/6/section/309/enacted> accessed 17 August 2017.

229 The Companies Act 2006 <www.legislation.gov.uk/ukpga/2006/46/contents> accessed 17 August 2017.

230 A Keay, 'Good Faith and directors' duty to promote the success of their company' (2011) 32(5) The Company Lawyer 138-143.

231 S Sheikh, *A Guide to The Companies Act 2006* (Routledge 2013) 371.

1985; the Company Directors Disqualification Act 1986[232]; and the Insolvency Act 1986[233]. With regard to the above, directors are legally bound to act for and on behalf of, or in the best interests of, the company for which they are conducting business. As fiduciaries, company directors are obliged to act *bona fide*[234] all the time.

6.1.2 Pre-existing Common Law and Section 309(1) of the Companies Act 1985 in Relation to Good Faith

In the 1988 company law case of *Brady v. Brady*[235] the court was concerned with what the 'company's interests' actually entailed and it dealt with whose interests that the company directors ought to consider. The court acknowledged the need for reform to ascertain their concerns.[236] Furthermore, under section 309(1) of the Act 1985, the company directors were legally bound to pay attention to the 'interests of the company's employees in general, as well as the interests of its members'[237]. Hence, for Alcock, the Act 1985 mandated that directors' duty to act in 'good faith' was solely to have regard for 'the interests of its members'[238]. This study maintains that there is no stipulation in the Act 1985 as to whose interests were primary or the most important. Following the latter, this study argues that the discretion of the company directors was too wide and that reform was needed to give some more clarity.

---

[232] The Company Directors Disqualification Act 1986 <www.legislation.gov. uk/ukpga/1986/46/section/6> accessed 17 August 2017.

[233] The Insolvency Act 1986 <www.legislation.gov.uk/ukpga/1986/45/ section/271> accessed 17 August 2017.

[234] S Sheikh (n 231) 373.

[235] *Brady v Brady* [1988] BCLC 20.

[236] Ibid 40.

[237] Companies Act (1985) c6 s309 <www.legislation.gov.uk/ukpga/2006/46/ section/172> accessed 17 August 2017.

[238] A Alock, 'An accidental change to directors' duties?' (2009) 30 Company Lawyer 368.

The reform came in a body of a new Companies Act in 2006. However, before this study turns to the analysis of the Act 2006 and its representation of the 'good faith' concept, it will look briefly at the case law and the historical development of the *bona fide* rule under English law.

6.1.3 Historical Development of the Company Directors Duty of Good Faith under English Case Law

The classical moment in the history of company directors' duty to act in 'good faith' took place in the 1942 company law case of *re Smith and Fawcett Ltd*[239] where the court held that court decisions in respect of the company directors' acts ought to be analysed from the perspective of what the directors consider - not what a court may consider - is in the best interests of the company.[240] This indicates that the requirement of 'good faith' makes it necessary that the interests of the company hold first place and company directors should not place their own interests before those of the company. Furthermore, in the 2001 company law case of Regentcrest *Plc v. Cohen*[241], Jonathan Parker LJ suggested that directors' duty to act in 'good faith' in the best interests of the company is based on the director's state of mind.[242] Hence, company directors will not be held to have not believed that they were acting in the best interests of the company, and consequently not in 'good faith', just because it may appear to the court that the company directors' belief was unreasonably held.[243] This line of reasoning is upheld by the ruling of the 2003 company law case

---

[239] *Re Smith & Fawcett Ltd* [1942] Ch 304.

[240] Ibid 306.

[241] *Regentcrest plc v Cohen* [2001] 2 BCLC 80.

[242] Ibid.

[243] Ibid 120.

of *Extrasure Travel Insurance Ltd v. Scattergood* [244] where the court held that what counts is the company directors' *honest belief* that their actions were in the best interest of the company. The court upheld the previous courts opinions that the courts' view about what would be best for the company is irrelevant.[245] Nonetheless, it is up to company directors to convince the court that they were acting in 'good faith' to promote the best interest of the company. If they are successful, there is a high probability that courts will not find them liable.[246]

In addition, courts must distinguish what the company directors have done from what the court feels they ought to have done.[247] In the 1883 company law case of *Hutton v. West Cork Rly Co*[248] the court stated that '*bona fides* cannot be the sole test, otherwise you might have a lunatic conducting the affairs of the company, and paying its money (...) in a manner perfectly *bona fide*, yet perfectly irrational'[249]. The court continues '[a] principle which must be tuned to the wavelength of the directors' conscience may be welcome to a theologian but will be of little significance as a legal control'[250]. Consequently, the subjective test of whether the company directors' acted in 'good faith' or not creates some concerns but there are at least two situations where a court can consider objective matters when testing the company directors' acts of 'good faith' in the best interest of the company.[251]

---

[244] *Extrasure Travel Insurance Ltd v Scattergood* [2003] 1 BCLC 598.

[245] Ibid 87, 90.

[246] A Keay, 'Good Faith and directors' duty to promote the success of their company' (2011) 32(5) The Company Lawyer 138-143.

[247] R Parsons, 'The Director's Duty of Good Faith' (1967) 5 Melbourne University Law Review 395, 417.

[248] *Hutton v West Cork Railway Co* (1883) 23 Ch D 654.

[249] Ibid 671.

[250] Ibid.

[251] Ibid.

The first situation was identified in the 1970 company law case of *Charterbridge Corp Ltd v Lloyds Bank Ltd*[252] where the court held that where the company directors (against whom the complaint had been initiated) had actually breached the duty to act in 'good faith' for the benefit of the company, the court had to first ascertain whether an intelligent and *honest person* in the same position could, taking into consideration all the conditions connected with or relevant to the conduct, have a *reasonable belief* that this conduct was in the best interests of the company.[253] It was asserted that where company directors turn their mind to whether conducting the action in question was in the best interest of the company, then the court ought to focus on the company directors' subjective 'good faith' alone.[254]

The second situation is derived from the assumption where the company directors against whom the proceedings have been initiated had *believed* that their actions were in the best interests of the company. The courts, however, are not legally bound to trust the company directors' statements. Therefore, the court can question the company directors' statement. For example, in the 1988 company law case of *Company (No.00370 of 1987), Re*[255] the judge pointed out that courts are not obliged to accept the company directors' declaration stating that they acted in 'good faith' without questioning it, if the courts have sufficient grounds to dispute the company directors' *honest belief*.[256] Subsequently, in the 2003 company law case of *Extrasure Travel Insurance Ltd v*

---

[252]   *Charterbridge Corp Ltd v Lloyds Bank Ltd* [1970] Ch 62.

[253]   Ibid 74.

[254]   See, for example, *Extrasure Travel Insurance Ltd v Scattergood* [2003] 1 BCLC 598 at 91; *Smitel Communications Ltd in Liq* (No 3)(1992) 7 ACSR 176.

[255]   Company (No 00370 of 1987), Re [1988] BCLC 570.

[256]   Ibid 577.

Scattergood[257] the court maintained that the fact that the company director's alleged beliefs was *unreasonable* may provide evidence that it was not in fact honestly held at the time'[258]. The *reasonableness* of company directors' conduct seems to have an important role when the courts define and agree on whether the company directors breached their duty to act in 'good faith' in the best interests of the company or not. For example, in the 2004 company law case of *Item Software (UK) Ltd v Fassihi*[259] the court held that 'there is no basis on which Mr. Fassihi [the director] could *reasonably* have come to the conclusion that it was not in the interests of [the company] to know of his breach of duty'.[260] The court held that the duty was not breached by the Mr. Fassihi's conduct and the *reasonableness criteria*, became relevant when considering whether the company director acted in 'good faith'.[261] Now this study turns to the analysis of directors' duty of 'good faith' in the best interests of the company from the perspective of the Companies Act 2006.

6.1.4 Company Directors' Duty of Good Faith under The Companies Act 2006

It was 8 November 2006, when for the first time in English law history the general duties of company directors had been set out in the Act 2006 which provides what the objective of the company directors' conduct should be.[262] Section 172(1) of the

---

[257] *Extrasure Travel Insurance Ltd v Scattergood* [2003] 1 BCLC 598; Also, see *Advance Bank v FAI Insurances* (1987) 12 ACLR 118 at 137; *Whitehouse v Carlton Hotel Pty Ltd* (1987) 11 ACLR 715 at 721.

[258] Ibid 90.

[259] *Software (UK) Ltd v Fassihi* [2004] EWCA Civ 1244.

[260] Ibid 44.

[261] A Keay, 'Good Faith and directors' duty to promote the success of their company' (2011) 32(5) The Company Lawyer 138-143.

[262] A Keay, 'Section 172(1) of the Companies Act 2006: an interpretation and assessment' (2007) 28 The Company Lawyer 106 – 110.

Act 2006 reads that the company directors must act in the way they consider would be the most likely to promote the success of the company for the benefits of its members and the company directors' consideration must be undertaken in 'good faith'.[263] The Explanatory Notes on Key Clauses suggest that company directors' decisions in respect of how to promote the company success and what contributes to the company success is left for company directors' 'good faith' judgment.[264] It states further that it will ensure that business decisions on, e.g. strategy and tactics are for company directors, and not subject to decision by the court, but are subject to 'good faith'.[265]

Still there are no definite standards against which the conduct of company directors can be assessed. As a consequence, company directors can merely express that their acts were in 'good faith', and their position then 'becomes virtually unassailable'.[266] In the face of these words, as long as the director acts in 'good faith', what matters is the director's view, not that of the courts – and the courts are unable to substitute their own judgment for that of the director. As argued previously, however, the courts[267], when considering the claims against the company directors as to whether they acted in breach of their duty to act *bona fide* in the best interests of the company, introduced an objective test to supplement the subjective one. The court in the 1970 company law case of *Charterbridge Corp Ltd v Lloyds Bank Ltd*[268] held that courts have the right to ask whether an intelligent and *honest person* in the same position of the director of the company involved 'could, in the whole

---

[263] The Companies Act 2006 (n 229).

[264] Explanatory Notes to the Companies Act 2006 at para 325 <www.legislation.gov.uk/ukpga/2006/46/pdfs/ukpgaen_20060046_en.pdf> accessed 17 August 2017.

[265] Ibid 327.

[266] Ibid.

[267] *Charterbridge Corp Ltd v Lloyds Bank Ltd* [1970] Ch 62.

[268] Ibid.

circumstances, have *reasonably* believed that the transaction was for the benefit of the company'[269].

Worthington suggests that the relevant case law should be taken into consideration as a guideline to the proper application of the law.[270] Furthermore, section 170(3) and (4) of the Act 2006 states expressly that 'the general duties are based on certain common law rules and equitable principles'[271]. Consequently, as argued by the author of this study, the company directors' duties should be interpreted, analysed and applied in the same manner as common law rules and equitable principles.[272]

In light of the above, company directors have the fiduciary duty to act in 'good faith' in the best interest of the company. In other words, the interests of the company and its shareholders are of primary importance. Hence, if company directors make a decision in the interests of the company, but contrary to the interests of one of the other constituencies, the company directors will not be in breach of duty. Cabrelli argues that as long as company directors are able to show that they considered these statutory factors, they will be able to prove that they acted accordingly with their obligations.[273] Furthermore, Cabrielli points out that courts are reluctant to interfere in the business decisions of company directors unless there is clear *dishonesty* and there is no reason to believe that this approach will change in the future.[274]

---

[269] Ibid 75.

[270] S Worthington, 'Reforming Directors' Duties' (2001) 64 Modern Law Review 439, 456.

[271] Companies Act 2006 s 170(3) and (4) <www.legislation.gov.uk/ukpga/2006/46/section /172> accessed 17 August 2017.

[272] Ibid.

[273] D Cabrelli, 'The Reform of the Law of Directors' Duties in UK Company Law' (2008) Presentation at Bocconi University, Milan, Bocconi University, Milan, Italy 18.

[274] Ibid 17.

Both case law and statutory law indicate that in most cases the courts would postulate that company directors are acting in 'good faith', unless the plaintiff can show evidence that indicates they are not, or unless the company directors' actions were so *unreasonable* that no *reasonable person* would have done the same thing in that situation. Hence, as noted, reasonableness or a reasonable person could define the act of 'good faith'. Would this mean that the breach of the duty to act in 'good faith' may be defined by the person's (e.g. company director) unreasonableness or his/her unreasonable actions? This line of reasoning would introduce the basic question, which is: what is reasonableness? What does it mean to be a reasonable person from the perspective of English common law? To find the answers to the above questions, this study will now turn to the idea of reasonableness. Just a caveat here, reasonableness will be analysed from the common law perspective. This is according to the directions of the section 170(3) and (4) of the Act 2006 that states expressly that 'the general duties are based on certain common law rules and equitable principles'.[275]

---

[275] Companies Act (2006) (n 271).

CHAPTER 7

REASONABLENESS AND HONESTY UNDER ENGLISH LAW

7.1 The Concept of the Reasonable Person under English Law

For Saltman, English Law has been laboriously built on the mythical figure of the 'Reasonable Man'.[276] In the field of jurisprudence, this legendary individual occupies the place which in another science is held by the Economic Man[277], and in social and political discussions by the Average or Plain Man[278]. Dowling even suggested that no matter what the particular department of human life may be which falls in to the consideration of courts, sooner or later we have to face the question: was this or was it not

---

[276] M Saltman, *The Demise of the Reasonable Man: A Cross-Cultural Study of a Legal Concept* (Transaction Publishers 1991) 4.

[277] JS Mill, 'On the Definition of Political Economy, and on the Method of Investigation Proper to It' London and Westminster Review in, *Essays on Some Unsettled Questions of Political Economy* (2nd edn, Longmans, Green, Reader & Dyer 1836).

[278] RE Dowling, 'Political Philosophy and the Plain Man' (1960) 19(3) Australian Journal of Public Administration 264-269.

the conduct of a reasonable man (reasonable person)?[279] In a study by Bongiovani, Sartor and Valentini, reasonableness or a reasonable person has taken a central place in English common law for quite a while. These scholars asserted that the reasonable person is neither a typical nor an average person and must not be confused with the rational person which acts only for his/her own interest. [280] Scanlon suggests that the concept of the reasonable person ought to be interpreted as an idea of fair terms of social cooperation.[281] This study takes a middle ground position and reasons that the reasonable company director is the one who acts in the best interests of the company and by doing so, he/she follows the idea of reasonableness.

When talking about reasonableness, this study takes an objective approach and not the company directors' subjective point of view. Let me elaborate on this assumption. Rawls posited that a reasonable person is motivated by a wish for a social world in which he/she being free and equal, and is able to act together with others on terms all can accept, so that each benefits along with others.[282] Accordingly, we may differentiate the rational company director, who acts in a way that is the best for his/her personal situation, from the reasonable company director, who takes the proper interest in the company affairs and acts in the best interests of the company.

With the above in mind, Wierzbicka argues that a reasonable person sets the standard of behaviour by which anyone's behaviour can - and should - be judged.[283] This standard,

---

[279] AP Herbert, *Look Back And Laugh* (House of Stratus 2014) 77.

[280] G Bongiovanni and G Sartor and Ch Valentini, *Reasonableness and Law* (Springer Science & Business Media 2009) 255.

[281] TM Scanlon, *What We Owe Each Other* (Harvard University Press 1998) 192-197.

[282] J Rawls, *Political Liberalism* (Columbia University Press 1993) 50.

[283] A Wierzbicka, *English: Meaning and Culture* (Oxford University Press 2006) 108.

however, is not based on any empirical studies of most peoples' actual behaviour. This standard is a hypothetical one.[284] Luntz, Hambly and Hayes argue that the standard of the reasonable person is most of the time an idealised and ethical one, rather than the conduct of the actual 'man on the street'.[285] For Wierzbicka, any courts' knowledge based on the hypothetical judgment of a reasonable person can be analysed or interpreted as 'probabilistic, limited, fallible'.[286] The above reasoning may shed light on the reasons why the courts in England so often take a non-interventionist attitude when dealing with company directors' acts of *bona fide*.[287] Both the subjective nature of the *bona fide* rule or the probabilistic, limited, and fallible nature of the concept of the reasonable man have encouraged the courts' position of reluctance to interfere with company directors' business decisions. Consequently, as argued by Luntz, Hambly and Hayes, the logic of reasonableness or a reasonable person is never definitive or absolute and always depends on the circumstances.[288] To elaborate more in depth on the issue the next section will look at the case law example of the reasonableness test that was undertaken by the English court in the 1970 company law case *Charterbridge Corp Ltd v. Lloyds Bank Ltd*[289]

---

284 Ibid.

285 H Luntz and D Hambly and R Hayes, *Torts: Cases and Commentary* (Butterworths 1985).

286 A Wierzbicka (n 283) 108.

287 See, for example, *Charterbridge Corpn Ltd v Lloyds Bank Ltd* [1970] Ch 62; *Evans v Brunner Mond & Co Ltd* [1921] 1 Ch 359.

288 H Luntz and D Hambly and R Hayes, *Torts: Cases and Commentary* (Butterworths 1985) 156-157.

289 *Charterbridge Corpn Ltd v Lloyds Bank Ltd* [1970] Ch 62.

7.2 *Charterbridge Corp Ltd v Lloyds Bank Ltd* [1970] Ch 62 Test of the Intelligent and Honest Man as a Company Director

In the 1970 company law case of *Charterbridge Corp Ltd v. Lloyds Bank Ltd* a land development company (Castleford Ltd) that was owned by Mr. and Mrs. Pomeroy, was also one of a group of companies.[290] Castleford's directors manage the company to guarantee the indebtedness of another group company called Pomeroy Ltd. Eventually, the company was approved to grant a legal charge over certain elements of its property to secure the guarantee. The Castleford directors were of the same mind that when doing so they had considered the interests of the whole group and not separately thought about the interests of Castleford itself. During the proceedings the court took into consideration whether or not the directors had acted in accordance with their duty to act in 'good faith' in the best interests of the company.

The court held that after reviewing the case, the directors of Castleford considered the interests of the whole group and no special regard had been given to Castleford itself. Therefore, the company directors must be treated as not having performed with a view to the benefit of Castleford itself. Furthermore, the court found that only if the company directors would address their mind specifically to the interest of the company in connection with each particular transaction would this represent a breach of the duty to act in 'good faith' in the best interests of the company. Pennycuick LJ summarised the facts as set out above and continued:

> 'The proper test, I think, in the absence of actual separate consideration, must be whether an intelligent and honest man in the position of a director of the company concerned, could

---

[290] Ibid.

in the whole of the existing circumstances, have reasonably believed that the transaction was for the benefit of the company. If that is the proper test, I am satisfied that the answer here is in the affirmative.'[291]

The court stated that Castleford looked to Pomeroy for its own day-to-day management and that the collapse of Pomeroy would have been a disaster for Castleford. Therefore, the court was satisfied with Castleford's director, who took an objective view in the exclusive interest of Castleford at the date of the guarantee.

The 1970 *Charterbridge Corp Ltd v Lloyds Bank Ltd*[292] case argues that the company director's lack of success in considering the company's best interest will not always result in the director breaching his duty to act in 'good faith' in the company's best interest. As the company director did not take into consideration the company's interest, in such circumstances, an objective 'test of [an] intelligent and honest man as company director'[293] standard must be applied. By the same token, honesty as part of reasonableness takes an important place during the process of courts' consideration as to whether the company directors fulfilled their duty to act in 'good faith' and in the best interests of the company or whether the company directors were in breach of that duty.

The next part of this study will briefly consider the concept of an *honest man* and its interpretation from the perspective of English common law. The English common law perspective will be applied and assumed to be applicable to the interpretation of the concept of the 'honest man' in a similar way as it happened with regard to the concept of 'reasonableness' following the directions of the

---

[291] Ibid 74.

[292] Ibid.

[293] Ibid.

section 170(3) and (4) of the Act 2006 that states expressly that 'the general duties are based on certain common law rules and equitable principles'.[294]

7.3 The Concept of the Honest Man under English Case Law

The issue that must be considered now is whether the company director against whom a petition is filed can claim that he/she is not liable because he/she believed that his/her conduct was not fraudulent. On the other hand, such a statement from the company director might not be enough and another standard to interpret his/her acts would be applicable. In the 1982 criminal law case of *R v Ghosh*[295] dealing with dishonesty, deception, theft and considering prosecution for acquiring property by deception in breach of the Theft Act 1968[296], the court held that whether the defendants acted dishonestly depends upon whether they acted in a way that would be interpreted by ordinary people as dishonest. In addition, as stated by the court, it is not relevant whether the defendants asserted that they believed that they were acting in a morally justified way.[297]

In the *1986 R v Lockwood*[298] fraudulent trading case, the Court of Appeal held that the judgment and interpretation of dishonesty

---

[294] Companies Act (2006) (n 271).

[295] *R v Ghosh* [1982] QB 1053.

[296] The Theft Act 1968 is an Act of the Parliament of the United Kingdom. It creates a number of offences against property in England and Wales. On 15 January 2007 the Fraud Act 2006 came into force, redefining most of the offences of deception <www.legislation.gov.uk/ukpga/1968/60/contents> accessed on 17 August 2017.

[297] *R v Ghosh* [1982] QB 1064.

[298] *R v Lockwood* [1986] 2BCC 99, 333.

given in the *R v Ghosh*[299] case was of general application.[300] As argued by Keay in two other civil cases, (1995 *Royal Brunei Airlines Sdn Bhd v Tan*[301] and 2002 *Twinsectra Ltd v Yardley*[302]) the courts took into consideration the issue of dishonesty consistent with the interpretation given in *R v Ghosh*[303]. However, in these cases, the respondents were involved in dishonestly assisting a breach of trust. This study does not concentrate in-depth on each of this cases but only aims to see what they have to say about the concept of the 'honest man.'

7.3.1 *Royal Brunei Airlines Sdn Bhd v Tan* [1995] 2 AC 378 and *Twinsectra Ltd v Yardley* [2002] UKHL 12 and The Concept of the Honest Man

In the 1995 *Royal Brunei Airlines Sdn Bhd v Tan*[304] case, Lord Nicholls considered that 'acting dishonestly, or with a lack of probity, which is synonymous, means simply not acting as an honest person would in the circumstances'[305]. Following the above, Pearce, Stevens, and Barr argued that honesty is not an optional scale, with higher and lower values according to the moral standards of each individual and that any assessment of dishonesty needs to be contextual and take account of the circumstances of the transaction.[306] Furthermore, His Lordship stated that an honest person does not 'deliberately close his eyes and ears, or deliberately not ask questions, lest he learn something he would rather not

---

[299] *R v Ghosh* [1982] QB 1064.

[300] *R v Ghosh* [1982] QB 99, 340.

[301] *Royal Brunei Airlines Sdn Bhd v Tan* [1995] 2 AC 378.

[302] *Twinsectra Ltd v Yardley* [2002] UKHL 12.

[303] *R v Ghosh* [1982] QB 1064.

[304] *Royal Brunei Airlines Sdn Bhd v Tan* [1995] 2 AC 378.

[305] Ibid 389.

[306] Pearce, R and Stevens, J and Barr, W, *The Law of Trusts and Equitable Obligations* (Oxford University Press 2010).

know, and then proceed regardless'[307]. Likewise, in the 2002 *Twinsectra Ltd v Yardley*[308] case, Lord Slynn held that 'prima facie, shutting one's eyes to problems or implications and not following them up may well indicate dishonesty'.[309]

Subsequently, this study will analyse the above words from the perspective of company directors' duty to act in 'good faith' in the best interests of the company. We may assume that an honest company director is required not to deliberately close his/her eyes when acting or when preforming his duties. If the company director closes his/her eyes or deliberately does not ask questions, lest he learn something which he/she would rather not know, and then proceeds regardless, he/she might be in breach of the duty to act in 'good faith' in the best interests of the company. Interestingly for this study, deliberately closing one's eyes to problems or implications and not following them up from Shaw's perspective constitutes company directors' acts of wilful blindness.[310] For Show, when company directors intentionally avoid finding out about a situation or act that will incriminate them, this means that these company directors are acting with their 'eyes shut'.[311] Nonetheless, this study indication of the relationship between company directors' dishonest acts of bad faith (falling foul of their duty to act in 'good faith') from the perspective of the 'wilful blindness' doctrine will not be complete without an actual overview of the 'wilful blindness' doctrine from the perspective of English law itself.

The next section of this analysis will briefly focus on a short introduction to the concept of 'wilful blindness' under English law. Information about applications of 'wilful blindness' doctrine under

---

[307] *Royal Brunei Airlines Sdn Bhd v Tan* [1995]2 AC 378.
[308] *Twinsectra Ltd v Yardley* [2002] UKHL 12.
[309] Ibid 4.
[310] P Shaw, *E-Business Privacy and Trust: Planning and Management Strategies* (John Wiley & Sons 2002) 79.
[311] Ibid.

English criminal and civil (non-criminal) law will be taken into consideration. Furthermore, this study will undertake an exposition of dishonest assistance[312] arguing that dishonest assistance makes it possible to conduct a cross-application, between the 'wilful blindness' doctrine and the breach of a duty to act in 'good faith' for the best interest of the company from the perspective of company directors' dishonest conduct.

Before the author proceeds, a caveat. Directors may incur personal liability, both civil and criminal, for their acts or omissions of 'good faith' in directing the company. It is beyond the scope of this study, however, to list all the various matters for which directors can be held to be liable. This study aims to elaborate on the company directors' breach of their duty to act in 'good faith' for the best interest of the company while acting dishonestly, arguing that while doing so the company directors can act with their 'eyes wide shut'. In light of the above, this study suggests that some of the company directors' acts of bad faith (falling foul of their duty to act in 'good faith') may be cross applied with the acts of wilful blindness.

---

[312] Dishonest assistance, or knowing assistance, is a type of third party liability under English trust law. See: S Elliot and C Mitchell, 'Remedies for Dishonest Assistance' (2004) 67 Michigan Law Review 16. Form more information, see S Elliot and C Mitchell, 'Remedies for Dishonest Assistance' (2004) 67 MLR 16.

CHAPTER 8

THE DOCTRINE OF WILFUL BLINDNESS UNDER ENGLISH LAW

8.1 Introduction to Wilful Blindness under Criminal and Civil English Law

'Wilful blindness' is a legal concept that is used as a means of drawing an inference about what a person (e.g. company director) knew, most often where there is some doubt about that person's honesty.[313] The 'wilful blindness' doctrine has been applied as a concept both in English criminal and civil law.[314] From the perspective of the English criminal law, wilful blindness has been described as connivance.[315] In the 1861 criminal law case of *Gipps v. Gipps and Hume*[316], Lord Westbury stated that conniving is not

---

[313] See, for example, *Royal Brunei Airlines Sdn Bhd v Tan* [1995] 2 AC 378; *Twinsectra Ltd v Yardley* [2002] UKHL 12.

[314] See, for example, *Gipps v Gipps and Hume* (1861) 11 HL Cas 1; *Economides v Commercial Union Assurance Co Plc* [1997] EWCA Civ 1754, [1998] QB 587.

[315] *Gipps v Gipps and Hume* (1861) 11 HL Cas 1.

[316] Ibid.

a narrow interpretation of wilfully refusing to see, or intending not to see or become acquainted with, that which a person knows or believes is taking place, or will happen. It must be consistent with a person's acceptance of something reluctantly but without protest. Therefore, it refers to wilfully abstaining from taking any steps to prevent what passes before the person's eyes.[317]

In the 1970 *Huckerby v. Elliot*[318] criminal law case, the court held that where a company director connives in the offence committed by the company, he is equally well aware of what is going on but his agreement is tacit, not actively encouraging what happens but letting it continue and saying nothing about it.[319] Subsequently, Williams has argued that wilful blindness, from the perspective of criminal law, is an 'unstable' rule[320] nevertheless, it is a rule that has been commonly applied in proceedings where an accessory[321] has been found to have the same *mens rea* as the principal offender.[322] The concept is also put to use in relation to statutory conspiracies[323], anti-money laundering[324] and company law[325].

---

[317] Ibid.

[318] *Huckerby v Elliott* [1970] 1 All ER 189.

[319] Ibid 194.

[320] G Williams, *Criminal Law the General Part* (Stevens & Sons 1953) 158 para 56.

[321] Accessory in legal use has been defined as someone who gives assistance to the perpetrator of a crime, without directly committing it. See: S Rapalje and RL Lawrence, *The Lawbook ExchangeA Dictionary of American and English Law* (The Lawbook Exchange, Ltd 1888) 11.

[322] Ibid (n 320) 395 para 132.

[323] See, for example, *Westminster CC v Croyalgrange Ltd* [1986] 1 WLR 674.

[324] See, for example, *Shah v HSBC Private Bank (UK) Ltd* [2010] EWCA Civ 31; *Abou-Rahmah and others v Abacha and others* [2006] EWCA Civ 1492.

[325] See, for example, Financial Services and Markets Act 2000 section 397 <www.legislation.gov.uk/ukpga/2000/8/section/397> accessed 17 July 2017.

Within an English civil law frame of reference, the 'wilful blindness' doctrine takes its place among the laws relating to non-disclosure in insurance contracts[326], the tort of misfeasance in public office[327] and of dishonest assistance in the breach of fiduciary duties.[328] The concept may additionally come into play where a fiduciary seeks the consent of his or her principal in what otherwise would be a breach of fiduciary duty – in which case the fiduciary cannot blindly assume that the principal to whom the duty is owed has been fully informed so that the consent to the breach is real.[329] In addition, as argued by Hannigan, the courts have established that a third party who received company funds might be liable to the company if he/she received the funds with knowledge of the company directors' breach of duty, whether it be actual knowledge, or knowledge in the sense that he/she wilfully shut his/her eyes to the obvious, and failed to make the type of inquiries which 'an honest man would have made'.[330] Hannigan sets out the basis of a claim for dishonest assistance.

---

[326] See, for example, *Economides v Commercial Union Assurance Co Plc* [1997] EWCA Civ 1754, [1998] QB 587.

[327] See, for example, *Three Rivers District Council and Others v. Governor and Company of The Bank of England* [2000] UKHL 33; [2000] 3 All ER 1; [2000] 2 WLR 1220.

[328] *Royal Brunei Airlines v Tan* [1995] 2 AC 378; *Smith New Court v Scrimgeour Vickers* [1997] AC 254; *Corporacion Nacional del Cobre De Chile v Sogemin Metals* [1997] 1 WLR 1396; *Fortex Group Ltd v MacIntosh* [1998] 3 NZLR 171; *Wolfgang Herbert Heinl v Jyske Bank* [1999] Lloyd's Rep Bank 511; *Thomas v Pearce* [2000] FSR 718; *Grupo Toras v Al-Sabah* (2000) unreported, 2 November CA; *Twinsectra v Yardley* [2002] 2 All ER 377.

[329] See, for example, *Bank of Credit and Commerce International (Overseas) Ltd v Akindele* [2000] EWCA Civ 502.

[330] B Hannigan, *Company Law* (Oxford University Press 2012) 292; For more see: *Eagle Trust Plc v SBC Securities Ltd* [1993] 1 WLR 484; *Selangor v United Rubber Estates Limited v Cradock* (No 3) [1968] 2 All ER 1073; *Eagle Trust plc v SBC Securities Ltd* [1992] 4 All ER 488; *Re*

Following the reasoning of this study, cases of dishonest assistance make it possible for the 'wilful blindness' doctrine and the breach of a duty to act in 'good faith' in the best interests of the company to be cross-applied from the perspective of company directors' dishonest conduct. In view of the above, this study focuses on the requirements for the claim of dishonest assistance and its overview. Before continuing, for ease of reference, the term 'breach of trust' shall stand for 'breach of any fiduciary duty', and the term 'beneficiary' shall stand for 'any person who takes a benefit from any fiduciary duty'.[331]

8.2 Dishonest Assistance when the Potential Exists for Cross-Applying Doctrines such as the Wilful Blindness and Bad Faith of Company Directors' Dishonest Conduct Exists

As argued by Hudson, any person who assists in a breach of a fiduciary duty, will be personally liable to account to the beneficiaries of that fiduciary duty for any loss caused by that breach of duty if the defendant has acted dishonestly.[332] For Hudson, dishonest assistants are those who may be held liable for dishonest assistance in a breach of fiduciary duty, which may include 'employees of companies who direct the activities of such companies' (company directors).[333] In claims of dishonest assistance there are two requirements for the defendant's liability. The first is

Montagu's Settlement Trust [1992] 4 AII ER 308; *Polly Peck International plc v Nadir (NO2)* [1992] 4 AII ER 769; *Covan de Groot Properties Ltd v Eagle Trust plc* [1992] 4 AII ER 700.

331 *Dubai Aluminium v Salaam* [2002] 3 WLR 1913; [2003] 1 All ER 97 para 9.

332 A Hudson, 'Liability for dishonest assistance in a breach of fiduciary duty' (2007) Journal of Trust and Corporate Planning 1.

333 Ibid.

that the defendant must have assisted in the breach of trust. The second condition is that the defendant assistance must have been dishonest.[334] To understand the dishonest assistance case the author creates an imaginary scenario.

Second Hypothetical Scenario: Dishonest Assistance Case

There are two companies, airline company A (appellant) and travel agency company B. There was an agreement between them that B company was to sell tickets for A company. Company B held money for the sale of tickets on express trust for company A in a current account. Furthermore, the current account has been used to defray some of B company's expenses. Company B was required to account to company A for this money within one month. The respondent who was the managing director and principal shareholder of company B, was Mr. Director. Amounts were occasionally paid out of the current account into deposit accounts that were controlled by Mr. Director. B company held the proceeds of the sale of tickets as trustee for A company (appellant). B company went into insolvency and as a consequence A company sought to proceed against Mr. Director for knowingly assisting in a breach of trust.

The above hypothetical scenario has its equivalent in a real life scenario which will be analysed in the next part of this study.

---

[334] A Hudson (n 332) and Ibid (n 328).

8.2.1 *Royal Brunei Airlines v Tan [1995] 2 AC 378* and Dishonest Assistance

In the 1995 trust law[335] case *Royal Brunei Airlines v. Tan*[336], Royal Brunei Airlines appointed Borneo Leisure Travel (BLT) to be its agent for booking passenger flights and cargo transport around Sabah and Sarawak. BLT's managing director and main shareholder was Mr. Tan. Money that was received for Royal Brunei Airlines was supposed to be held on trust in a separate account until passed over. However, BLT, with Mr. Tan's assistance, paid money into its current account and used it for its own business. BLT failed to pay on time, the contract was terminated, and the company became insolvent. Royal Brunei Airlines claimed the money back from Mr. Tan.[337] The court stated that Mr. Tan was liable as a constructive trustee to Royal Brunei Airlines. The Court of Appeal of Brunei Darussalam held that the company was not guilty of fraud or dishonesty, and therefore Mr. Tan could not be either.[338] The case was appealed to the Privy

---

[335] English trust law. A trust is an equitable obligation, binding a person (who is called a trustee) to deal with property over which he has control (which is called the trust property) for the benefit of persons (who are called beneficiaries) of whom he himself may be one and any of whom may enforce the obligation. The essence of a trust is that the concept of ownership is divided: the trustee is given the legal title to the property which gives them the duty to manage and control the property for the benefit of the beneficiaries who are exclusively entitled to the benefit of the property. For more information see: JE Martin, *Hanbury & Martin: Modern Equity* (19th edn, Sweet & Maxwell 2012) 49.

[336] *Royal Brunei Airlines v Tan* [1995] 2 AC 378.

[337] Ibid.

[338] In English law, the word constructive trustee means that if A dishonestly assists B to commit a breach of trust, A will be held liable for the losses arising from the breach of that trust as a 'constructive trustee'; For more information see: L Smith, 'Constructive trusts and constructive trustees' (1999) 58 Cambridge Law Journal 294.

Council. It was held by Nicholls LJ that it was Mr. Tans's; it was the dishonest assistant's state of mind which mattered. Knowledge depends on a 'gradually darkening spectrum'[339]. Therefore the test for being liable in assisting breaches of trust must depend on dishonesty, which is objective. Furthermore, Lord Nicholls held that it is irrelevant what the primary trustee's state of mind is, if the assistant himself is dishonest. Therefore, the accessory is to be fixed with personal liability for the breach.[340]

Lord Nicholls created a test of 'dishonesty'. Stating that acting dishonestly means simply not acting as an honest person would in the circumstance, and claimed that this is an objective standard. [341] His Lordship continued that a dishonest person deliberately closes his/her eyes, or deliberately does not ask questions, lest he/she learn something he/she would like to know, and then proceeds regardless. Thus these phrases, which have been referred to in the above case, relate to a person (here, a dishonest assistant; Mr. Tan managing company director) who deliberately does not make an enquiry about a fraudulent matter of which he has suspicion. In view of the above, and referring back to the points made previously, it becomes noticeable that these same conditions of the 'dishonest' test are required while questioning company directors' acts of 'good faith' in the best interests of the company cases. In addition, the grounds or the foundations on which the 'dishonest' test have been created constitute a 'wilful blindness' doctrine. Consequently, the author argues that the company directors' dishonest breach of their duty to act in 'good faith' for the best interest of the company in question can be cross-applied with the act of wilful blindness.

---

[339] Ibid (n 336).
[340] Ibid.
[341] Ibid.

PART IV

CONCLUSION

CHAPTER 9

PROPOSED MODE OF JUDICIAL REVIEW OF GOOD FAITH

9.1 Proposed Mode of Judicial Review of Good Faith in England

The purpose of this study was to examine the company directors' duty to act in 'good faith' in the best interests of the company. Furthermore, this analysis was aimed at discussing the possibilities of cross-application between the doctrine of 'good faith' and the doctrine of 'wilful blindness' from the company directors' perspective. The issues were explored through analysis of Delaware in the United States and English legislation, case law and relevant secondary sources. The laws of Delaware and England are very similar in respect of the obligations of company directors to act in 'good faith' in the best interests of the company.

However, they are relatively different when it comes to the interpretation of the company directors' duty to act in 'good faith' in the best interests of the company. Differences can also be observed in terms of the consequences of the business judgment rule that is present in Delaware, USA but not in English, UK jurisprudence. The business judgment rule is a regulation that helps to make sure that company directors are protected from misleading allegations about the way in which they conduct business.[342] Unless it is apparent that the company directors blatantly violated some major rule of conduct, the courts will not review or question their decisions or dealings.[343] For company directors to be able to take justified risks in the course of business management, company directors should enjoy sufficient freedom and any unreasonable liability associated with risk-taking should be eliminated. It goes without saying that risk-taking is a central aspect of the company directors' role.[344]

The business judgment rule is intended to limit the liability of company directors in order to enable them to take reasonable risks to promote business growth without the fear of losing their personal assets in the case of failure. Without the business judgment rule, courts have to dig into the reasons for company directors' decisions, assessing their conduct from the point of view of a hypothetical reasonable person. Within English jurisprudence, hypothetical reasonableness, or the reasonable company director, is the one who acts in the best interests of the company and who, by doing so, follows the idea of reasonableness.[345]

Nevertheless, as pointed out by Wierzbicka, this standard of reasonableness is a hypothetical one.[346] Therefore, the knowledge of the courts about company directors' actions when in question is based on hypothetical judgment and consequently, is limited and

---

[342] EP Welch, AJ Turezyn, RS Saunders, *Folk on the Delaware General Corporation Law 2014: Fundamentals* (Publisher Aspen Publishers Online 2013) 139.

[343] Ibid.

[344] AR Pinto, DM Branson, *Understanding corporate law* (LexisNexis Matthew Bender 1999) 187.

[345] TM Scanlon, *What We Owe Each Other* (Harvard University Press 1998) 192-197.

[346] A Wierzbicka (n 283) 108.

fallible. Therefore, in England, the subjective nature of the *bona fide* rule and probabilistic nature of the concept of reasonableness has perhaps made the courts reluctant to interfere with company directors' business decisions, narrowing the courts' opinions and interpretations of falling foul of the duty to act in 'good faith'.

Nonetheless, as argued by this study, there are legal cases in English jurisprudence which, when analysing company directors' acts of 'good faith', apply a test of a reasonable and honest man.[347] It requires the court to test whether an intelligent and honest man in the position of a director of the company concerned, could, in the whole of the existing circumstances, have reasonably believed that the transaction was for the benefit of the company.[348] The author finds that for a person (e.g. company director) to act dishonestly under English case law means to deliberately close his/her eyes and ears, or deliberately not ask questions, lest he/she learn something he/she would rather not know, and then proceed regardless.[349] As this study argues further, the process of deliberately closing company directors' eyes to problems or implications of their decisions and not following them up constitutes not only acts of dishonesty but also acts of wilful blindness. [350]

The doctrine of 'wilful blindness' is a legal concept used in criminal and civil law as a means of drawing an inference about what a person knew, and most often where there is some doubt about that person's honesty.[351] Therefore, the author favours the opinion that, under English jurisprudence, there is a possibility of cross-application of the doctrine of 'good faith' with the doctrine

---

[347] See, for example, *Charterbridge Corpn Ltd v Lloyds Bank Ltd* [1970] Ch 62
[348] Ibid 74.
[349] See, for example, *Royal Brunei Airlines Sdn Bhd v Tan* [1995]2 AC 378; *Twinsectra Ltd v Yardley* [2002] UKHL 12 at 4.
[350] P Shaw, *E-Business Privacy and Trust: Planning and Management Strategies* (John Wiley & Sons 2002) 79.
[351] See, for example, *Royal Brunei Airlines Sdn Bhd v Tan* [1995]2 AC 378; *Twinsectra Ltd v Yardley* [2002] UKHL 12.

of 'wilful blindness' from the perspective of company directors' conduct. However, the following circumstances need to be met (a) the company director must have assisted in the breach of trust which stands for the breach of any fiduciary duty; and (b) the assistance of the defendant, in this case the company director must have been dishonest.[352] The following conditions set out the basis of a claim for dishonest assistance.

As pointed out by Hannigan, the courts established that the company directors who received company funds may be liable to the company if they received the funds with knowledge of their breach of duty, whether it was actual knowledge or knowledge in the sense that the company directors 'wilfully shut their eyes to the obvious and did not make any inquiries which an honest person would have made'.[353] As a result of this, the author concludes that, under English jurisprudence, in the event of company directors receiving company funds and dishonestly assisting in a breach of trust while wilfully shutting their eyes to the obvious may be cross-applied with the falling foul of the duty to act in 'good faith' in the best interests of the company.

9.2 Proposed Mode of Judicial Review of Good Faith in Delaware

In Delaware the judicial review of the 'good faith' doctrine proceeds differently to the one in England, UK. In Delaware, USA the duty of loyalty calls for company directors to act in good faith in the best interests of the company. The company directors' subjective motivation is needed for the courts to decide whether or not their acts were in 'good faith'.[354] The company directors' motivation can be concluded from the circumstances of the business decision and

[352] *Dubai Aluminium v Salaam* [2002] 3 WLR 1913; [2003] 1 All ER 97 para 9.
[353] B Hannigan, *Company Law* (Oxford University Press 2012) 292.
[354] As the discussion above attests.

from the essence of the decision itself.[355] Furthermore, as noted, in Delaware, USA under the business judgment rule, a plaintiff when showing that company directors were acting in a direct or indirect financial self-interest, may prove that the company directors' were falling foul of the duty to act in 'good faith'. In the absence of direct or indirect self-interest the company directors are assumed to act in 'good faith'. Still, the plaintiff may question the company directors' 'good faith' by showing that the essence of the company directors' decision or conduct itself failed to give a true notion of the presumption that they were acting in 'good faith'. It would require the court to take into consideration the probable result to be achieved by the company directors' decision or conduct. To do this, the plaintiff would have to prove that the company directors were involved in a relationship with persons who stood to benefit from the company directors' decision and that, viewed in light of the facts as they were actually known or wilfully blindly known by the directors at the time the decision was made, the decision would be of greater benefit to those persons than to the corporation. If the company directors were unable to show the decision was motivated by a valid corporate purpose, it would follow that it was motivated by a purpose other than the best interests of the corporation, namely the interests of another constituency. That would establish a violation of the duty of loyalty which calls upon company directors to act in 'good faith'.

In addition, the author establishes that recklessness or deliberate indifference has been included under the umbrella of 'good faith'.[356] The author recognises further that even the doctrine of 'wilful blindness' may be a suitable one to create an interpretative basis for the falling foul of the duty to act in 'good faith' from

---

[355] CW Furlow, 'Good Faith, Fiduciary Duties and the Business Judgment Rule in Delaware' (2009) Utah Law Review 1061.

[356] HA Sale, 'Delaware's Good Faith' (2004) 89 Cornell Law Review 456 and J Edwards, 'The Criminal Degrees of Knowledge' (1954) 17 Modern Law Review 294, 298.

the perspective of company directors' conduct. By making this recognition the author gradually analyses this line of thought by primarily focusing on Sale's approach who provides an in depth analysis of the recklessness concept (as understood by the federal securities law) that could be cross-applied with company directors' acts of 'good faith.' This study takes this thought further by pointing out that recklessness as understood by the securities law has its origins in common law. This is a direct outcome of the 1978 securities law case of *Roolf v. Blyth, Eastman Dillon & Co., INC* and the court judgement where it was held that '[It] is unquestionable that the common law has served as an interpretive source of securities law concepts'.[357] Following this line of reasoning, the author establishes that under the common law a reckless defendant (e.g. company director) has been recognised as the one that does not possess actual knowledge because he/she is understood as not conscious of the existence of a fact that can be proved by subjective evidence.[358]

These findings lead this study to further arguments supporting its case by turning to the 1964 securities law case of *United States v. Benjamin,* where the court recognises that reckless defendant is the one who deliberately closes his/her eyes to facts he/she had a duty to see.[359] Subsequently, this research argues that the company director falling foul of the duty to act in 'good faith' is the reckless actor who acts with the awareness of the high probability of the existence of a fact but wilfully shuts his/her eyes to the facts which he/she has a duty to take into consideration. The court's reasoning in the *United States v. Benjamin* echoes wording of the Model Penal Code Section 2.02(7), which states that the defendant (e.g.

---

[357] *Roolf v Blyth, Eastman Dillon & Co,* INC 570 F2d 38, 45 (1978).

[358] HAL Hart, *Punishment and Responsibility Essays in the Philosophy of the Law* (Clarendon Press 1975) 152.

[359] *United States v Benjamin* 328 F2d 854, 862 (2d Cir 1964).

company director) who has 'virtually certain knowledge'[360] or so-called awareness of the need for some more inquiry but declines to make the enquiry because he/she does not wish to face the consequences of the truth has been described as committing acts of wilful blindness.[361] Consequently, this study, supported by Robbins' opinion that the high-probability language of the MPC's definition of wilful blindness indicates recklessness[362], has argued that the falling foul of the duty to act in 'good faith' from the perspective of company directors' conduct may be cross-applied with the doctrine of wilful blindness as understood by the MPC.

[360] JL Marcus, 'Model Penal Code Section 2.02(7) and Willful Blindness' (1993) 102(8) The Yale Law Journal 2235-36.

[361] Ibid.

[362] I Robbins, 'The Ostrich Instruction: Deliberate Ignorance as a Criminal Mens Rea' (1990) 81 Journal of Criminal Law and Criminology 223.

CONCLUSION

On 14 August 2014, the author of this study received the following e-mail from Professor HA Sale, the first scholar who successfully cross-applied the doctrine of 'good faith' from the perspective of company directors' conduct with recklessness under the Delaware jurisdiction:

> 'I do think it is possible to cross-apply the doctrines [the doctrine of 'good faith' and the doctrine of 'wilful blindness']. Delaware has really narrowed 'good faith' since the time I wrote that piece ['Delaware's Good Faith' article][363]. As a result, the doctrine really doesn't have teeth at this point.'[364]

Subsequently, the above opinion is a framing support for the findings of this study with regard to Delaware jurisprudence. As noted, however, Delaware, US and English, UK Company Laws differ respectively. The author argues that Under English jurisprudence the doctrines' cross-application is only possible

---

[363] Professor HA Sale is talking about the following article: HA Sale, 'Delaware's Good Faith' (2004) 89 Cornell Law Review 456.

[364] HA Sale, (personal communication, 14 August 2014).

in the author's opinion in specific circumstances, namely the company directors' dishonest assistance cases. This analysis does not exclude other possibilities of the cross application of the breach of the company directors' duty to act in 'good faith' in the best interests of the company and the doctrine of 'wilful blindness'. Nonetheless, it was not the author's aim to analyse all the other possibilities for when applications can be made under these two doctrines in the same proceedings. In summary, this study provides evidence which suggests that there are some important links between the company directors' duty to act in good faith in the best interests of the company and the doctrine of 'wilful blindness.'

This study only begins to reveal the potential of cross application between these two doctrines and takes into consideration the company directors' perspective. Based on these results, the author provides recommendations for future research. Some questions which remain unanswered have been exposed in the course of undertaking this endeavour such as the connection between the business judgment rule and the process of judicial review of 'good faith' from the perspective of company directors' conduct. Furthermore, should the business judgment rule be adopted in English jurisprudence? In England, UK except for dishonest assistance circumstances, what are the other possibilities when the doctrine of 'good faith' and the doctrine of 'wilful blindness' in the same proceedings can apply?

Based on the findings the author argues that there are legal instruments in both Delaware, USA and English, UK legal systems that if appropriately employed could reduce the risks of the company directors falling foul of the requirements of 'good faith' while deliberately 'closing their eyes' to obvious warning signs.

'Either (…) this was in effect a cover - up, or you weren't told, or you didn't read your e-mails properly, and there is a failure of governance within the company. Do you accept that?'[365]

Barrister Robert Jay QC asked James Murdoch this question in the Leveson Inquiry into the culture and ethics of the press. Murdoch's answer was, in essence, that his direct reports kept him in the dark. The biggest threats and dangers the company faces are the ones the company directors don't see – not because they are secret or invisible, but because they are wilfully blind. The author hopes that this analysis will inspire potential readers to undertake further research and continue with establishing ways to ensure that company directors are 'wilfully awaken' in the best interest of the company.

---

[365] Leveson Inquiry into the Culture, Practices and Ethics of the Press <www.levesoninq uiry.org.uk/> accessed 17 August 2017

BIBLIOGRAPHY

Legislation

Delaware General Corporation Law (Title 8, Chapter 1 of the Delaware Code) <http://delcode.delaware.gov/title8/c001/index.shtml> accessed 17 July 2017

Model Penal Code 2.02(7) (official and Revised Comments 1985)

Securities Exchange Act of 1934 <www.sec.gov/about/laws/sea34.pdf> accessed 17 July 2017

The Companies Act 2006 (c 46) <www.legislation.gov.uk/ukpga/2006/46/contents> accessed 17 July 2017

The Cuban Assets Control Regulations, 31 CFR 515

The Trading with the Enemy Act of 1917 (40 Stat 411, enacted 6 October 1917, codified at 12 USC § 95a et seq)

Secondary Sources

Books

Anderson, TL and Sousa, R, *Reacting to the Spending Spree: Policy Changes We Can Afford* (Hoover Press 2013)

Arsalidou, D, *Objectivity vs. Flexibility in Civil Law Jurisdictions and the Possible Introduction of the Business Judgment*

Rule in English Law (Sweet and Maxwell Limited and Contributors 2003)

Berle, AA and Means, GC, *The Modern Corporation and Private Property* (2nd edn, Brace and World 1967)

Bongiovanni, G and Sartor, G and Valentini, Ch, *Reasonableness and Law* (Springer Science & Business Media 2009)

Brownsword, R, *Good Faith in Contract: Concept and Context* (Ashgate Publishing Group 1999)

Cartwright, A, *Mixed Emulsions: Altered Art Techniques for Photographic Imagery* (Quarry Books 2011)

Cherry, RL, *Title English Words: From Latin and Greek Elements* (University of Arizona Press 1986)

Choper, JH, *Cases and Materials on Corporations* (6th edn, Aspen Publishers 2004)

Clarke, T, *International Corporate Governance: A Comparative Approach* (Routledge 2007)

Cross, F and Miller, R, *The Legal Environment of Business: Text and Cases -- Ethical, Regulatory, Global, and E-Commerce Issues* (Cengage Learning 2008)

CTI Reviews, *The Legal and Regulatory Environment of Business: Business, Business law* (15th edn, CTI Reviews 2016)

De Lacy, J, *Reform of UK Company Law* (Routledge 2013)

Dubber, MD, *Criminal Law: Model Penal Code* (Foundation Press 2002)

Gross, H, A *Theory of Criminal Justice* (Oxford University Press 1979)

Gruner, RS, *Corporate Criminal Liability and Prevention* (Law Journal Press 2004)

Halpin, A, *Definition in the Criminal Law* (Hart Publishing 2004)

Hart, HAL, *Punishment and Responsibility Essays in the Philosophy of the Law* (Clarendon Press 1975)

Hazen, TL and Markham, JW, *Corporations and Other Business Enterprises* (West 2003)

Heller, K and Dubber, M, *The Handbook of Comparative Criminal Law* (Stanford University Press 2010)

Hannigan, B, *Company Law* (Oxford University Press 2012)

Herbert, AP, *Look Back And Laugh* (House of Stratus 2014)

Herring, J, *Criminal Law: Text, Cases, and Materials* (Oxford University Press 2004)

Horrigan, B, *Corporate Social Responsibility in the 21ˢᵗ Century: Debates, Models and Practices Across Government, Law and Business* (Edward Elgar Publishing 2010)

Judge, S, Q & A *Revision Guide: Company Law 2012 and 2013* (Oxford University Press 2012)

Keay, A, *Company Directors' Responsibilities to Creditors* (Routledge 2007)

Keay, A, *The Enlightened Shareholder Value Principle and Corporate Governance* (Routledge 2012)

Keeton, WP, *Prosser and Keeton on the Law of Torts* (5ᵗʰ edn, West Group 1984)

Kershaw, D, *Company Law in Context: Text and Materials* (Oxford University Press 2012)

Kipnis, K, *Philosophical Issues in Law: Cases and Materials* (Prentice Hall College Div XI 1977)

Lane, MJ, *Representing Corporate Officers, Directors, Managers, and Trustees* (2ⁿᵈ edn, Aspen Publishers Online 2013)

Loughrey, J (ed), *Directors' Duties and Shareholder Litigation in the Wake of the Financial Crisis* (Edward Elgar Publishing 2013)

Luntz, H and Hambly, D and Hayes, R, Torts: *Cases and Commentary* (Butterworths 1985)

Martin, JE, *Hanbury & Martin: Modern Equity* (19ᵗʰ edn, Sweet & Maxwell 2012)

McPhail, TL, *Global Communication: Theories, Stakeholders and Trends* (John Wiley & Sons 2013)

Mill, JS, 'On the Definition of Political Economy, and on the Method of Investigation Proper to It' London and Westminster Review in, *Essays on Some Unsettled Questions of Political Economy* (2ⁿᵈ ed, Reader & Dyer 1836)

O'Connor, J, *Good Faith in English Law* (Dartmouth Publishing 1990)

Pachecker, HH, *Nafa's Blue Book: Legal Terminology, Commentaries, Tables and Useful Legal* (Xlibris Corporation 2010)

Pearce, R and Stevens, J and Barr, W, *The Law of Trusts and Equitable Obligations* (Oxford University Press 2010)

Pearsall, J, *New Oxford Dictionary of English* (Oxford University Press 2001)

Pinto, AR, Branson, DM, *Understanding corporate law* (LexisNexis Matthew Bender 1999)

Quinton, AM, *Knowledge and Belief*, in *The Encyclopedia of Philosophy*, Volume 4

Rapalje, S and Lawrence, RL, *The Lawbook Exchange A Dictionary of American and English Law* (The Lawbook Exchange, Ltd 1888)

Rawls, J, *Political Liberalism* (Columbia University Press 1993)

Roberts, R, *The City: A Guide to London's Global Financial Centre* Volume 11 of The Economist (John Wiley & Sons 2008)

Rubin, R and Babbie, ER, *Essential research methods for social work* (2nd edn, Brooks-Cole 2010)

Saltman, M, *The Demise of the Reasonable Man: A Cross-Cultural Study of a Legal Concept* (Transaction Publishers 1991)

Scanlon, TM, *What We Owe Each Other* (Harvard University Press 1998)

Shaw, P, *E-Business Privacy and Trust: Planning and Management Strategies* (John Wiley & Sons 2002)

Sheikh, S, *A Guide to The Companies Act 2006* (Routledge 2013)

Usa Ibp Usa (ed), *Us Company Laws and Regulations Handbook Volume 2 Delaware - Corporate Laws and Regulation in the Selected States of the Us Delaware* (Int'l Business Publications 2009)

Vetri, D et al, *Tort Law and Practice* (5th edn, Carolina Academic Press 2016)

Welch, EP, Turezyn, AJ, Saunders, RS, *Folk on the Delaware General Corporation Law 2014: Fundamentals* (Publisher Aspen Publishers Online 2013)

Wierzbicka, A, *English: Meaning and Culture* (Oxford University Press 2006)

Williams, G, *Criminal Law. The General Part* (2nd edn, Sweet & Maxwell 1961)

Dictionaries

American Heritage Dictionary of the English Language (4th edn, Houghton Mifflin Harcourt 2000)

Journal Articles

Alock, A, 'An accidental change to directors' duties?' (2009) 30 Company Lawyer

Bainbridge, SM, 'The Business Judgment Rule as an Abstention Doctrine' (2004) 57 Vanderbilt Law Review

Berry, MR, 'Does Delaware's Section 102(b)(7) Protect Reckless Directors From Personal Liability? Only if Delaware Courts Act in Good Faith' (2004) 79 Washington Law Review

Bolger, JP, 'Recklessness and the Rule 10b-5 Scienter Standard after Hochfelder' (1980) 49(5) Fordham Law Review

Buell, S, 'In What Is Securities Fraud?' (2011) 61 Duke Law Journal

Burgman, DA and Cox, PN, 'Corporate Directors, Corporate Realities and Deliberative Process: An analisis of the Trans Union Case' (1986) 11 Journal of Corporation Law

Butler, HN, and Ribstein, LE, 'Opting Out of Fiduciary Duties: A Response to the Anti- Contractarians' (1990) 65 Wash L Rev

Cabrelli, D, 'The Reform of the Law of Directors' Duties in UK Company Law' (2008) Presentation at Bocconi University, Milan, Bocconi University, Milan, Italy

Charlow, R, 'Wilful Ignorance and Criminal Culpability' (1992) 70 Texas Law Review

Chesnut, KL, 'Comment, U.S. v. Alvaredo: Reflections on a Jewell' (1989) 19 Golden Gate University Law Review

DeMott, D, 'Puzzles and Parables: Defining Good Faith in the MBO Context' (1990) 25 Wake Forest Law Review

Dowling, RE, 'Political Philosophy and the Plain Man' (1960) 19(3) Australian Journal of Public Administration

Easterbrook, FH and Fischel, DR, Contract and Fiduciary Duty (1993) 36 J L & Econ

Edwards, J, 'The Criminal Degrees of Knowledge' (1954) 17 Modern Law Review

Eisenberg, MA, 'The Duty of Good Faith in Corporate Law' (2006) 31 Delaware Journal of Law

Elliot, E and Mitchell, C, 'Remedies for Dishonest Assistance' (2004) 67 MLR

Furlow, CW, 'Good Faith, Fiduciary Duties and the Business Judgment Rule in Delaware' (2009) Utah Law Review

Griffith, SJ, 'Good Faith Business Judgment: A Theory of Rhetoric in Corporate Law Jurisprudence' (2005) 55(1) Duke Law Journal

Haimoff, L, 'Holmes Looks at Hochfelder and 1Ob-5,' (1976) 32(147) Business Lawyer

Holland, RJ, 'Delaware Directors' Fiduciary Duties: The Focus on Loyalty' (2009) 11 The University of Pennsylvania Journal of International Business Law

Hudson, A, 'Liability for dishonest assistance in a breach of fiduciary duty' (2007) Journal of Trust and Corporate Planning

Hurt, C 'The Undercivilization of Corporate Law' (2007) U Illinois Law & Economics Research Paper No LE07-005

Husak, DN and Callender, CA, 'Wilful Ignorance, Knowledge, and the 'Equal Culpability' Thesis: A Study of the Deeper Significance of the Principles of Legality' (1994) Wisconsin Law Review

Jennings, RW, 'Federalization of Corporate Law: Part Way or All the Way'(1976) 31 Business Lawyer

Keeton, P, 'Fraud: The Necessity for an Intent to Deceive' (1965) 5 University of California at Los Angeles Law Review

Keay, A, 'Good Faith and directors' duty to promote the success of their company' (2011) 32(5) The Company Lawyer

Keay, A, 'Section 172(1) of the Companies Act 2006: an interpretation and assessment' (2007) 28 The Company Lawyer

Keay, K, 'The Duty to Promote the Success of the Company: Is It for Purpose?' (2010) University of Leeds School of Law, Centre for Business Law and Practice Working Paper <http://ssrn.com/abstract=1662411> accessed on 17 July 2017

Krawiec, KD, 'Corporate Decisionmaking: Organizational Misconduct: Beyond the Principal-Agent Model' (2005) 32 Florida State University Law Review

Lowell, AD and Arnold, KC, 'Corporate Crime after 2000: A New Law Enforcement Challenge or Deja Vu' (2003) 40 American Criminal Law Review

Luban, D, 'Contrived Ignorance' (1999) 87 Georgia Law Journal

Marcus, JL, 'Model Penal Code Section 2.02(7) and Wilful Blindness' (1993) 102(8) The Yale Law Journal

Mann, RA and Roberts, BS *Essentials of Business Law and the Legal Environment* (Cengage Learning 2012)

Nowicki, EA, 'A Director's Good Faith' (2007) 55 Buff L Rev

Parsons, R, 'The Director's Duty of Good Faith' (1967) 5 Melbourne University Law Review

Perkins, RM, '"Knowledge" as a Mens Rea Requirement' (1978) 29 Hastings L

Rapp, GC, 'The Wreckage of Recklessness' (2008) 86 Wash U L Rev

Reed, JL and Neiderman, M, 'Good Faith and the Ability of Directors to Assert § 102(b)(7) of the Delaware Corporation Law as a Defense to Claims Alleging Abdication, Lack of

Oversight, and Similar Breaches of Fiduciary Duty' (2004) 29 Delaware Journal of Corporate Law

Robbins, IP, 'The Ostrich Instruction: Deliberate Ignorance as a Criminal Mens Rea' (1990) 81 Journal of Criminal Law and Criminology

Robinson, PH, 'The American Model Penal Code: A Brief Overview' (2007) 10 New Criminal Law Review

Sale, H, 'Delaware's Good Faith' (2004) 89 Cornell Law Review

Smith, L, 'Constructive trusts and constructive trustees' (1999) 58 Cambridge Law Journal

Stewart, F and Mervyn, L, 'The Capacity for Recklessness' (1992) 12 (74) Legal Studies

Stout, LA, 'Type I Error, Type II Error, and the Private Securities Litigation Reform Act' (1996) 38 Arizona Law Review

Strine Jr, LE, 'Can We Do Better by Ordinary Investors? A Pragmatic Reaction to the Dueling Ideological Mythologists of Corporate Law' (2014) 2(114) Columbia Law Review

Summers, RS, 'Good Faith in General Contract Law and the Sales Provisions of the Uniform Commercial Code' (1954) 54 Virginia Law Review

Veasey, EN, 'State-Federal Tension in Corporate Governance and the Professional Responsibilities of Advisors' (2003) 28 Journal of Corporation Law

Worthington, S, 'Reforming Directors' Duties' (2001) 64 Modern Law Review

On-line Newspaper Articles

Burns, JF, 'Panel in Hacking Case Finds Murdoch Unfit as News Titan' *The New York Times* (1 May 2012) <www.nytimes. com/2012/05/02/world/europe/murdoch-hacking-scandal-to-be-examined-by-british-parliamentary-panel.html?page wanted=1&_r=2&hp&> accessed 17 July 2017

Davis, N, 'Rupert Murdoch: Scotland Yard want interview about crime at his UK papers' (*The Guardian*, 25 June 2014) <www.theguardian.com/uk-news/2014/jun/24/scotland-yard-want-interview-ch-phone-hacking> accessed 17 July 2017

Doodds, WK and Tusk, CM, 'Delaware Supreme Court Clarifies "Bad Faith" in Brehm v. Eisner *Dechert LLP* (1 June 2006) <www.dechert.com/files/Publication/20d04a76-2aa5-4909-9d0c-c929a3da6a30/Presentation/PublicationAttachment/b4c8a6ff-8d3e-4fca-a095-ca2eda323464/WCSL_Alert_6-06.pdf> accessed 17 July 2017

Olson, JF and Scanlon, MJ, 'SEC Targets Directors Who Ignore Red Flags' *Gibson Dunn* (14 March 2014) <www.gibsondunn.com/publications/pages/SECTargetsDirectorsWhoIgnoreRedFlags.aspx> accessed 17 July 2017

Papadimitriou, D, 'The coming 'tsunami of debt' and financial crisis in America' *The Guardian* (15 June 2014) <www.theguardian.com/money/2014/jun/15/us-economy-bubble-debt-financial-crisis-corporations> accessed 17 July 2017

Peston, R, 'The next financial crisis?' *BBC News* (2 July 2014) <www.bbc.co.uk/news/business-28126241> accessed 17 July 2017

Project Syndicate economists, 'Will London survive as a financial centre after Brexit?' (*The Guardian*, 26 April 2017) <www.theguardian.com/business/2017/apr/26/london-financial-centre-brexit-eu-paris-frankfurt-uk> accessed 25 July 2017

Chasin, C, 'Jerome Krantz and Gary Nadelman of DHB Industries Settle Accounting Fraud Allegations' *RISC* (12 November 2011) <www.risc-llc.com/2011/11/cary-chasin-jerome> accessed 17 July 2017

Wayne, L, 'How Delaware Thrives as a Corporate Tax Haven' (*The NY Times*, 30 June 2012) <www.nytimes.com/2012/07/01/business/how-delaware-thrives-as-a-corporate-tax-haven.html> accessed 17 August 2017

Wright, O and Burrelle, I and Hickman, M, and Milmo, C and Grice, A, Hacking scandal: is this Britain's Watergate? *The Independent* (9 July 2011) <www.independent. co.uk/news/uk/crime/hacking-scandal-is-this-britains-watergate-2309487.html> accessed 17 July 2017

Other online sources

Black Jr, LSB, 'Why Corporation Choose Delaware' (2007) Delaware Department of State <http://corp.delaware.gov/ pdfs/whycorporations_english.pdf> accessed 17 July 2017

Cable, V, 'Transparency & Trust: Enhancing the transparency of UK company ownership and increasing trust in UK business' (Gov.uk, April 2014) <www.gov.uk/government/ uploads/system/uploads/attachment_data/file/304297/bis-14-672-transparency-and-trust-consultation-response.pdf> accessed 17 July 2017

Explanatory Notes to the Companies Act 2006 < www.legislation. gov.uk/ukpga/2006/46/pdfs/ukpgaen_20060046_en.pdf> accessed 17 July 2017

Hudson, A, 'Liability for dishonest assistance in a breach of fiduciary duty' <www.alastairhudson.com/trustslaw/ DAMar07.pdf> accessed 17 August 2017

Sparks, AG and Hurd, SM and Hirzel, ST, 'Good Faith and the Walt Disney Company Derivative Litigation - Guidance for Directors of Delaware Corporations'<http://www.nacdfl.org/ Portals/0/Outline%20-%20Good%20Faith%20and%20 The%20Walt%20Disney%20Co.pdf> accessed 17 July 2017

Thomsen, LC, Speech by SEC Staff: Keeping up with the Smartest Guys in the Room: Raising the Bar for Corporate Boards (May 12, 2008) US Securities and Exchange Commission <www.sec.gov/news/speech/2008/spch051208lct.htm> accessed 17 July 2017